For Michael, Elizabeth and Sam

FINDING ASPERGER SYNDROME IN THE FAMILY -A BOOK OF ANSWERS

Clare Lawrence

Emerald Publishing

Emerald Publishing
Brighton BN2 4EG

ISBN 184716 008 5
ISBN 13: 978184716 008 9

Printed by Biddles Kings Lynn Norfolk

Cover design by Bookworks Islington

Whilst every effort has been made to ensure that the information contained within this book is correct at the time of going to press, the author and publisher can take no responsibility for the errors or omissions contained within.

Foreword

Meeting people with Asperger syndrome (AS), chatting to them, listening to them, and discussing AS with them is the best way for neurotypical (NT) people to begin to understand AS at an individual and global level. The more people you meet, and the more people you are able to communicate with, the better your chances are to develop a perspective more in line with the AS way of thinking, and it is always a fascinating and eye opening journey. However, many neurotypical people do not have the time or the opportunity to take this journey, so it's lucky that we have books to fall back on. Books can help to develop our understanding and assist us in creating a more AS perspective of the world, better enabling us to live and work alongside people with AS. Thus it is with great pleasure that I am able to introduce this text which has been written by a parent of a child with AS - parents, of course, being the experts second only to the individual themselves!

People with AS often end up being vilified by neurotypical people just for being themselves. We look at the individual's behaviour and judge it (using purely NT values) in a negative way. Simply because the individual with AS may not behave in the same way as an NT it is as if he is always in 'the wrong'. Surely, however, once a diagnosis has been made then we should realise that, by definition, behaviour is likely to be different? So why the judgemental 'NTs are better' attitude? I suspect that the answer to this is a lack of understanding rather than anything more sinister or discriminatory; I hope so, at least. This book goes some way in encouraging the reader not to look simply at behaviour in an NT fashion, but to see it from a differing, AS, perspective. In doing so it sheds light on what may otherwise appear to make little sense.

I do not have a child with AS. I have never undergone the process whereby I must seek a diagnosis for my child, and then cope with all the emotions that this entails. I have, however, had a lot of contact with a lot of parents over the years and have recognised that so many parents do not get the post-diagnostic support from 'professionals' that they should. All too often parents are left essentially to 'fend for themselves' or are given either minimal or inaccurate information about their child's AS. Certainly, those parents would welcome a book such as this in order to begin to make sense of the often bewildering behaviours of their son or daughter.

One of the things that I love most about autism and AS is that the behaviour of the individual, in my experience, *always* makes sense. It's a case of working out why that behaviour occurs and seeing the world as closely as possible through the eyes of the individual; once this has been achieved much can become clear. However, this is not an easy thing to do. The complexities of AS mean that it is often incredibly difficult to understand why an individual behaves in a way that an NT would deem 'odd'. By definition NTs think in an acutely different way to people with AS - so it is easy to understand why NTs can find it so difficult to understand. Sometimes acceptance is all that is needed if the underlying causes are too problematic to work out. After all, we all like to be accepted for *who* we are irrespective of whether people have a true understanding of *why* we are.

The questions posed in this book, and the answers, stem directly from individuals with AS. As we know, no two individuals will be the same - so it could be argued that even if the answer to a question is absolutely correct for one individual, there is little point using that answer to explain the behaviour of another, unrelated, individual. However, this is too simplistic and ultimately a dangerous road to go down. I think we can all learn from individual experience, even if that experience does not relate directly to the child or adult we have in mind. Every single individual with AS has a multitude to offer - not just to other people with AS, but to their families and friends. What Clare has done in this book is to use her extensive experience and understanding to introduce other parents to the complex world of AS, and to provide some possible answers to the myriad of questions that are likely to be asked. This is to be commended; moreover, the style in which she does it makes for exceptionally 'easy reading' and the positive way in which she presents AS is definitely worth the read in itself.

Pretty much every day at work I get asked questions about AS - from individuals, parents, and professionals. I do not have all (or even close to most) of the answers such is the complexity of AS and the surrounding issues. Knowledge and understanding is not easy to come by, and anything that assists in the development of either (or both) should be welcomed with open arms. Clare's 'book of answers' is not a complete guide to understanding your child; you are unlikely to have all the answers to all the questions you have ever had after having read it. However, it does go a long way towards identifying many of the issues that parents face on a daily basis, and provides intelligent and sound guidance that will benefit the reader.

Luke Beardon 2007

Finding Asperger syndrome in the family - a book of answers

Introduction

Four years ago we came away from receiving a diagnosis of Asperger syndrome (AS) for our son, Sam, with our heads reeling with questions. Some of those questions are here. In the intervening years I have talked to many people, particularly to parents newly facing a diagnosis (sometimes in a daughter, although more often in a son) and so other of these questions come from a kind of combined Asperger Child who emerges from us all.

One of those parents explained to me that part of her confusion came from the fact that she no longer felt that she knew her child. The experts who had given the label had, by doing so, seemed to understand her child's behaviour better than she did. The time from his birth until that point seemed to have been spent with one child; now she must let that person go and get to know this new, 'Asperger' child. This redrawing of the family map can be a difficult and painful process, and is one which is filled with questions. This book is for everyone coming to terms with that time. I hope it helps.

It is not a book which will give you bio-medical explanations for the ways your child's brain functions differently (there are plenty of those available already, if you can understand them!). What it will do is give you some insights into possible reasons why he behaves as he does, and some practical hints as to ways to help him, and the rest of the family, move on into the future with AS.

You may have spotted that the three 'big' questions ('Will he get better?' 'How did she get it?' 'How bad is it?) are at the end of the book. This is deliberate. I think it is easy to feel, when you first face this diagnosis, that these are the *only* questions. In fact, as time goes on they become less urgent as the enormity of the diagnosis becomes less overwhelming. Instead you begin to realise that the other questions- about understanding behaviour, about ways to help your child and about learning to live with Asperger syndrome in your family - are just as, if not more, important. The big three are still there; go straight to the end and read them if you like – but don't discount all the other 'little' questions. Some of these may never have occurred to you before. Some may be things you were wondering about long before an official diagnosis. They are questions which occur at the level where it is easiest to understand and to help your child. Perhaps they are not so small after all.

A note:

This book is about having Asperger syndrome, so why does it keep going on about autism? There has been a lively (and as yet inconclusive) debate in academic circles of recent years: Is Asperger syndrome the same as autism? Autistic Spectrum Disorder (ASD) or Autistic Spectrum Condition (ASC) are terms designed to cover a full range of conditions, usually (although not always) including Asperger syndrome. I use the term 'autism' frequently in this book quite deliberately. For the first year after Sam was diagnosed we used to tie ourselves into knots trying to avoid it – but in the end, it's only a word. Like 'Asperger', the more you say it, the less fearful it feels. My advice would be to say both ten times before breakfast; go to the bottom of the garden and shout them. Neither of them can hurt you if you don't let them!

Finding Asperger syndrome in the family: a book of answers

Section Three 83

What about the rest of us?
Living with AS in the family.

Finding Asperger syndrome in the family: a book of answers

Section One:
"Why does he do that?" Understanding your child's Asperger behaviour

……………………………………………………………………………

1. Why does he make so much fuss?

"Making a fuss" could, perhaps, be defined as 'minding about something which doesn't bother other people'. It doesn't matter to the majority of us whether the curtain edges are drawn *precisely* together, or whether we watch to the very end credits of a cartoon, or whether our baked beans touch our mashed potato. We may, therefore, view our child with Asperger syndrome's attitude on these matters as "making a fuss." Yet it might equally be said that we "make a fuss", as far as our children with AS are concerned, when we insist they keep their clothing on in public, remain seated in assembly or don't sing out-loud on the bus.

I think the problem here is different perceptions of what is important. If we show respect for what is important to our children with AS, regardless of whether we share that view, it is more likely that they will be more tolerant of the "fusses" we make. It is also important to note that however odd, frustrating, or bewildering the behaviours may seem to us, to the individual with AS they serve a very important and, often, sensible purpose–just because we don't know what it is doesn't mean it doesn't exist!

2. Why doesn't he make *any* fuss?

One of the more alarming aspects of AS can be that the child appears not to feel pain. He may fall over, knock himself, and show no signs of distress. He doesn't make a fuss about such things because they simply do not appear to hurt him.

It is now understood that many children with conditions on the autistic spectrum may experience sensory information differently to other people. This is crucial information for understanding behaviour. The child with AS may not volunteer information that he is in pain. It is for his parents or teachers, if his behaviour becomes erratic, if he is being 'difficult' or upset, to 'play the detective'. Close cross-questioning ("Do you have a pain in your tummy?" "Do you have a pain in your ear?") may frequently yield a surprised "yes", and a trip to the doctor will identify, perhaps, an ear infection. Clearly, an understanding of this sensory difference is essential in helping your child to manage his Asperger syndrome. Some individuals may not even be at the stage where they recognise that they are hurt at all, in which case 'playing the detective' becomes doubly important.

3. Why does he go on and on about things?

Obsessive repetition around the same subject can be fairly wearing on the family, but as with most things to do with AS, this going on and on is likely to be serving a useful purpose for your son. He may be taking refuge in repetition of facts about his 'special interest' in order to reduce his levels of stress – or he may just be enjoying spending some time on what interests him most. I think some acceptance of this sort of behaviour is best. You may not want to learn that much about the classification of fictional space vessels, but if your son is trying to share his interest with you, then surely that is worth something. It also gives you access to a motivator; if he enjoys telling you about these obscure facts then let him, if he has tidied his room first! We usually put a time limit on his monologue, depending on the context (if something stressful is happening then this is likely to be longer than if everything is calm.) We then try to turn the 'conversation' elsewhere. We don't want to shut down what is, after all, a form of communicating, but equally we don't want to accept that this is the best, or all, we are likely to get. (See Q 51 *'Should we go along with his current Special Interest?'*)

4. Why doesn't she look at me?

Lack of eye contact is frequently (but by no means always) found in children with AS. It may be because the child simply does not see any reason to look as well as listen, or it may be because looking directly into another person's eyes feels so intrusive that it is actually painful. Some programmes stress the need to encourage eye contact to improve social interaction, while other professionals (and many individuals with AS themselves) suggest that insisting on eye contact may actually interfere with the person's ability to interact. It is clear in some situations that to insist on eye contact is to decrease the individual's actual ability to process the information they need in order to interact, essentially reducing skills rather than improving them. In other cases peripheral vision may be better than 'head on' in which case while we assume that the individual is not looking, he may well be.

As with most things, perhaps the emphasis should be on the word 'encourage' and away from the notion of 'insist'. If you feel that your child really hasn't understood a need to look at or towards the speaker, then gentle encouragement to do so may help, particularly if insistence on looking into the eyes is avoided. It may help avoid accusations of 'not listening' in school if she learns that it is diplomatic to at least face towards the speaker. On the other hand, if she really does prefer not to make eye contact, and feels that she can listen better if looking elsewhere, than surely, with a little understanding from those around her, that can be accommodated. Teaching her tips such as 'watching the words come out of the mouth' or perhaps 'focussing on the bridge of the nose' may help her reach a compromise which is comfortable for all.

5. **Why does she still wet herself?**

Toileting problems remain some of the most difficult of those associated with the autistic spectrum - most difficult for the parents, for the siblings, for others and therefore ultimately for the self-esteem of the individual. Wetting or soiling yourself marks you as "different" in a uniquely unpleasant way. Unfortunately, these problems are also quite common in children with autism and Asperger syndrome and are likely to be due to a combination of sensory processing differences and problems with communication. The child may be unable to '-read-' the internal signs and doesn't realise she needs 'to go' until it is almost – or actually – too late, and when she does realise she may have difficulty in gaining an adult's attention or communicating the fact and its urgency. The good news is that she is likely to get better in time. Hard though it is, there is little to be done but to be patient, keep prompting her, don't make too big a deal of mistakes and remember that you are not alone. The supermarkets wouldn't sell age 8+ size Pull-Ups if it wasn't financially in their interest to do so, so they must sell a great many of them - to the neuro-typical population as well as to the Asperger.

6. Why can't he write?

Although by no means universal, problems with writing seem fairly common in children with AS. This may be because of an immature pencil grip, poor spatial processing, under-developed fine motor skills, a problem with audio processing… any number of reasons. It may help to find out why your child is struggling – and if you do, then there may be much you can do to help – but at the end of the day this may be something you (and he) need to learn to live with. Dr Tony Attwood, one of the foremost experts on Asperger syndrome (see contacts and further information at the end of this book), claims that handwriting is an outdated obsession that is about as useful today as being able to saddle a horse! In the end it may be best just to accept this weakness and concentrate on helping him to acquire keyboard computer skills instead. (See also Q72 *'If he's so clever, why's he doing so badly at school?'* and Q77 *'Is he dyslexic?'*)

7. Why doesn't she smile?

I think what this question means is: "why doesn't she smile at me?" After all, she probably does smile and laugh to herself when amused, excited, tickled etc., and may well do so at inappropriate times - such as when another child bangs his head. On the other hand, she may not use smiling as social intercourse. She may not smile back at someone who smiles at her, or smile to indicate pleasure at seeing her mother at the end of the school day. This does not indicate a gloomy personality, nor even lack of pleasure, but is more likely to be because she has not understood that a smile is a message. She has not realised that often we smile not because *we* are happy, but in order to *make the person smiled at* happy! Like most things this can be taught to ease social relationships (although there is a danger that a taught smile will remain a rather artificial smile), but she may never really see the need to do this spontaneously. I think this is a problem for us to deal with rather than being a problem directly for the child herself. It is well worth working out how your child does display affection and to grow to appreciate that, rather than always seeking neuro-typical forms of affection which may be less evident. (See also Q90 *'Doesn't he care when I cry?'*)

8. Why does he read so much?

The 'why' to this question is likely to be highly complex and perhaps best left to the psychologists to explain, but the fact remains that a seemingly large proportion of children with AS are highly fluent and enthusiastic readers. The great thing about this is that reading is a socially acceptable solitary pursuit, it is - or can be - highly educational, and it is QUIET! There are few contexts into which you might take your child within the adult world (a wedding ceremony, the dentist's waiting room, round to visit Great Aunt Flo...) where sitting quietly reading won't gain your child a huge number of Brownie Points. It is one answer to the question of how to survive much of school and it is one of the AS traits which has got to be most celebrated. Enjoy it!

9. Why is he such a messy eater?

Underdeveloped motor skills are common in children with AS. Getting food from plate to mouth using knife, fork and spoon is a skilful task, and it seems to take these children longer to master it than most. There is also an element of social pressure at work on children without AS to help them get it right – it is not 'nice' to be messy with your food after a certain age. This pressure to conform is likely to be weaker on the child with AS, who does not greatly notice the effect of his eating on those around him. He may also be interested in the texture of food – which may lead to a certain amount of food handling – or conversely he may be repulsed by the touch of metal to his mouth – which would lead to the same thing. As with so many things to do with AS, as a parent you may have to 'play detective' to find out what is happening with your particular child at this particular time before you can even begin to put it right. One of the keys then is to make sure that the child is motivated to do what you want him to do – which, generally speaking, won't be to please those around or to receive social praise. Make sure that the motivating factors are from his perspective, not yours.

10. Why doesn't he tell us what happened?

One aspect that makes a child with AS so vulnerable is this lack of 'telling tales'. It is as if what happened in the past has gone and has no bearing on the present. Yet many examples have shown that children with AS may possess exceptionally powerful memories.

The information is there, it is just not shared. Probably this is due to a deficit in social communication, an absence of the urge to share experiences merely as a social activity. It is, perhaps, another example of the lack of 'small-talk'. Be that as it may, it does lead to vulnerability.

Your child may not tell you that he has been thumped/teased/robbed unless you ask him directly. Clearly, since you are unlikely to know what has happened to him while he was away from you - for example at school - this can be tricky. A home/school diary to record important events can help greatly, in that it can share the positives as well as alerting you to the negatives. Your son may not think to tell you that he got top marks in a maths test, or that he was singled out for praise for his good behaviour and the diary allows you to bring these events to light and to celebrate them. Another technique is the use of the specific-general question. "Did anyone say "good" to you today?" Or, conversely, "Were you injured at all today?" These kinds of question may help to dig out what is going on in your child's life. (See also Q60 *'What should we do if she's bullied at school?'*)

11. Why does it take her so long to answer a question?

Children with AS may have problems processing information – particularly verbal information. If you ask your child a question you may almost be able to see her searching the files of her brain for the answer, and then forming that answer into a verbal response. The problem is that our typical reaction to a child not answering a question is to assume that she needs clarification and to rephrase it. The child with AS then has to start all over again with the new question, and the whole process begins again. Hard though it is, we need to accept that the answer may come more slowly in these children, and it may need a number of false starts, but that this does not mean that the answer is not there. Slow down and wait.

12. Why does she sometimes appear to be deaf?

It is not uncommon to find that parents have had their child's hearing checked early in investigations to find out why she is 'different' from other children. Her lack of turning to her parents' voices as a baby, her lack of response later to calls and questions, together with her slow or 'robotic' use of speech, could quite easily have suggested hearing loss (and it is only sensible to have this eliminated as a cause first.) In fact, although her hearing is fine, she may appear to be deaf - in a sense may actually BE deaf - when she is engrossed in another activity, particularly a visual one. Whereas most of us are able to filter information from other senses when using one (for example, getting 'lost' in a book or staring blindly into space when on the telephone) we retain the ability to register enough from the other senses to keep them useful. A child with AS's filtering system may, in a way, be too efficient. When reading, for example, her non-visual senses may be so effectively filtered out that she may genuinely not hear, smell or taste, feel heat or cold.

An understanding of this can help tremendously when dealing with her. Rather than yelling pointlessly at her and jumping up and down in fury because she is "ignoring you", it helps to understand that you need to get her attention, and to wait until that attention has truly shifted to you, before you make a request. It makes the world of difference!

13. Why can't he sit still?

Constant movement may be a sign that your child needs the sensory feedback from repositioning himself in space. The constant wriggling might be irritating but if you watch him closely you will probably find that he is doing it subconsciously and indeed that it is even an outward sign of inner thought. Try allowing him to kneel or stand to work, or try pushing a tennis ball onto one leg of his chair (the resulting 'wobble' may be all he needs to stay alert.) You could also try allowing breaks for physical activity when he is thinking – for example a few bounces on the trampoline, or just a trip to another room to fetch something you have 'forgotten'. Some therapists suggest the wearing of a weighted jacket may help the child to feel grounded (carrying a rucksack works too.) A less intrusive suggestion is probably to allow a 'twiddle object', a piece of soft tack or a small (tied) balloon half filled with flour for example, to aid concentration. The important thing to note is that usually the movements serve a very specific and useful purpose, so simply trying to stop the child is unlikely to work. (See Q38 *'Why buy her a trampoline?'*)

Incidentally, it is also worth investigating whether the wriggling is a result of other sensory distress – in other words, is he sitting on a pin, or is his bladder uncomfortably full? It's important not to over-look the obvious!

14. Why does he call out in assembly?

This could be put another way: why do head teachers (and the clergy - they also are guilty of this) insist on asking rhetorical questions? From the child with AS' viewpoint the response is completely understandable. A question has been asked, he knows the answer and so he gives it. The presence of the other x-hundred individuals is irrelevant. They didn't answer, so presumably they didn't know ...

A simple way round this, rather than teaching the concept of rhetoric at this stage, is to give rules as to where to speak and where to be silent. The problem is that this only partially solves the problem. Another place the answering of the not-to-be-answered question is likely to cause problems is in the realm of the classroom 'telling off'. You can scarcely encourage your child not to answer questions put directly by the teacher, yet "What do you think you are doing?", "Do you think I was born yesterday?" and "What do you think I am, stupid?" can, obviously, each be fraught with danger! To be serious, this does become a real danger as the child grows up. This mode of address, unfortunately, is favoured also sometimes by such professions as security guards or even the police. The consequences can be only too clearly imagined. (See Q 65 *'How do I stop him from getting into trouble?'*)

15. Why does he hate having his hair cut?

A visit to the hairdresser can be a nightmare for (and with!) a small child with a condition on the autistic spectrum. We are not the only family I've met who have been asked to leave a salon because of the screams of anguish coming from our child. The invasion of personal space, the smells, the sounds, the feel of the cut hair on neck and back - all seem to contribute to this being a particularly distressing experience for a child with autism.

So why did we do it? Why, when the experience clearly terrified our child, did we put a neat and respectable appearance above his well being? Perhaps it was because as parents we were already feeling under threat because our child was not developing 'normally'. Whatever the reason, it took us a long while to realise that we were getting our priorities a little out of order when we insisted on returning visit after disastrous visit to the hairdressing salon. The alternative was to buy trimmers and do a rather bad job of it ourselves, or to let his hair grow, like Samson, down to his ankles. We relented, accepting that the 'behaviour' was there for a reason. While we could assume to the ends of the earth that there is nothing frightening or worrying about getting our hair cut, we realised that we could not make this assumption on behalf of someone with AS. In fact, like many problems, as soon as we 'gave up', it sorted itself out. We took Sam with us when we all went to the hairdresser and let him sit in the corner reading a book, and after four or five visits he requested a haircut for himself. Perhaps one day we'll learn to trust his lead! (See Q63 *'How do we get him to the dentist?'*)

16. Why can't she follow instructions?

The answer is, of course, that she can – but that the way the instructions are given may need looking at. Verbal instructions are insubstantial. After you have said them they 'disappear' in that nothing concrete remains to remind the person. It may be helpful if you include visual prompts – either in written form or in the form of sequenced pictures. These break down a task into its component parts, and therefore make each part far easier to follow. "Get ready for school" as an instruction becomes a sequenced series of visual prompts, ordering what is required ('get your bag', 'pack your lunch', put on your shoes', fetch your homework') and in what order. In time this sequence becomes secure and the prompts can be phased out, although many people continue to find reassurance in breaking down a challenge into smaller, concrete steps (think how many of us faced with a difficult day begin by making a list.) And how many of us could follow the instruction "build the flat-packed book-case" without following the pictures? (See Q42 *'Why write her notes?'*)

17. Why does he roar like a tiger when he's angry?

Anger is an alarming emotion, both to witness and to feel. Many children with AS seem not to recognise the warning signs that they are becoming angry, and so appear to switch suddenly from calm to furious. These 'melt-downs' are distressing for everyone, not least for the child with AS, who must feel totally overwhelmed.

One way to help is to explore the early symptoms of anger with your child. Does he start to feel tense? Does he push his teeth together? Does he find that his hands squeeze together onto his fingers? Also important is to give your child a way of expressing that he is feeling these early signs (see *Q. 43 'What are Angry Cards?'*)

However, you may still find that your child 'borrows' expressions of anger, and of other emotions, from films, television or the computer. This is his way of finding a way to express emotions, and although it may appear slightly forced or artificial, the emotions are genuine. Roaring like a tiger may be an expression of anger which he has copied from a cartoon, but it is nevertheless valid.

18. Why is he so 'into' superheroes?

The great thing about super-heroes is that there is no moral ambiguity – and very little character development. Superheroes are good and super-villains are bad, and ultimately the good always conquers. Who wouldn't be attracted to such a universe?

For the child with AS this security must be very reassuring. He knows with whom he should identify, he knows what he would want to do in that position, he knows what is *right.* The real world is even more confusing to him than it is to the rest of us. He can't tell who is 'good' and who is 'bad', people can be kind one moment and angry the next, can say one thing and mean something else entirely. It is not surprising that a small boy with AS would want to be the big, strong hero who knows *exactly* what to do to save the day… and has the means to do it.

(Note: be careful about making sure that the child understands the difference between fact and fiction.

'Playing' at being a superhero is fine; actually thinking that you are one and have the power to fly, for example, is most categorically not!)

19. Why won't he let me give him a hug?

I think the answer to this may be in the wording of the question. Being 'given' a hug is to have something done to you, usually by someone bigger and stronger, and involves an element of capture or restraint. Put like that, it doesn't sound so attractive!

Work on getting to a point where your son *gives you* a hug. He may never want to; he may prefer to indicate the same affection by a high five, or even by a finger-tip-to-finger-tip action. Whatever gesture you eventually use to show affection, it must be voluntary, and it must be able to be instigated - and escaped from - by your son. (*See Q. 70 'Does that mean he'll never love us?'*)

20. Why does she push into queues?

The answer is most likely because she doesn't realise that the queue is there, or the purpose behind it has never been explicitly explained to her. Once it is pointed out to her that other people are waiting and that her turn is after the man in the green shirt, for example, there may not be a problem. However, if you are not with her and therefore not able to point this out to her, she is in danger of getting into difficulties. The sighs, clicked tongues and raised eyebrows, the expressions of "well, someone seems to be in a hurry" and so on are unlikely to mean much to her. As with so many things, the innocuous queue is fraught with danger for the individual with AS.

(See Q.62 *'Should we explain if she appears rude to strangers?')*

21. Why does he bump into people?

As mentioned before, children with AS may have poor spatial awareness and may not understand the concept of 'personal space' (see Q 66 *'How do I get him to understand about personal space?'*). They may stand uncomfortably close to someone they are talking to, or - for example - make everyone in a lift uncomfortable by standing at right angles to everyone else. This may explain the bumping ... or it may just be because it is fun. If you don't get any negative social feedback from doing it, you can see that bumping into people must have its plusses. You can see how strong you are, people make amusing grunts and squeaking noises when bumped, you get a nice bit of sensory feedback from the collision - in fact the whole thing is a lot like dodgem cars. Understanding all this is one thing, but you still have to stop it. Sometimes just telling the child that it is not allowed, and that continuing to do it will lead to the loss of some privilege or treat, is the only way. After all, we can't all go around having this much fun…!

22. Why doesn't he sleep much at night?

As far as I am aware, scientists are still researching why disturbed sleep patterns seem so prevalent amongst individuals with conditions on the autistic spectrum. The latest research seems to point towards altered levels of melatonin. Meanwhile, while scientists search for a reason and for a remedy, we as parents are left managing the nights. Steering a child with AS through the days can seem challenging enough; sleep deprivation may be the last straw.

Undoubtedly many parents do resort to sedative drugs, at least in the short term, to help manage the problem. This is one solution, especially in an emergency where the well being of the parent is seriously at risk. In the longer term, however, managing your child's wakefulness is likely to be a more satisfactory solution.

To be honest, it is not how much your child sleeps which matters (as long as he remains well). What matters is whether you get time when he does not need your attention, including sufficient time to sleep yourself. One advantage of his AS in this is that he is likely to be pretty self-sufficient, if given the opportunity. Given a good and changing supply of books around his special interest, possibly some toys, pens and pencils and a good supply of drawing paper he may well be happy to entertain himself. If you make rules very clear – for example, no coming downstairs after a certain time – you should be able to relax. If you don't feel you can switch off in case he starts wandering around the house after you are asleep, fit a motion sensor with an alarm on the stairs. Sometimes it pays to be pragmatic; he may not need to sleep, but you do - so do what you have to do to be confident that he is safe, and then grant yourself some time "off". (See Q29 *'Why does she like sleeping in a sleeping bag?'*

23. Why does she talk in a funny voice?

One early feature of AS is often a qualitatively 'odd' way of talking. The person may talk with a flat tone, lacking the ups and downs of natural speech. He may also miss the subtleties of communication, where a raised tone at the end of a comment changes it into a question, or where a pause after a comment indicates that it is a joke. Quite often this ties in with the next question (Q 24 *'Why does he say rude things?'*), since the tone may make what he says appear rude, even when the content is harmless. One way to teach that how things are said can be as important as what is said is to go through a sentence, emphasising each word in turn and looking at how that changes the meaning. Thus a simple sentence, "I need a drink", can have three meanings. "*I* need a drink" (never mind what anyone else needs), "I *need* a drink" (I'm getting desperate here) or "I need a *drink*" (not another sandwich). The game can be fun, and does help the child with AS to see that different emphasis on different words can radically change meaning. (See Q. 40 *'Why take him to a Speech and Language Therapist?*)

24. Why does he say rude things?

Interestingly, this is an example of something that is a problem to others, not to the young child with AS - yet. Your child is probably not embarrassed to ask the one-eyed stranger why his eye fell out, to tell his grandmother that her teeth are yellow or to inform his headmistress in assembly that she is in the wrong. It is important to remember that he is not being rude, just unaware of the effect of his curiosity or honesty on its recipient. Unfortunately, this is one of the ways that Asperger syndrome gets worse in time. It is just about acceptable for such remarks from a five-year-old, but not from a ten-year-old. As the child with AS gets older, his lack of social understanding makes him highly vulnerable. Youths hanging around on the park roundabout may find it funny when a toddler tells them that it is bad for them to smoke; they are unlikely to be so tolerant of the same lecture from an adolescent. The person with Asperger syndrome does not say rude things, but the person he speaks to may well *hear* rude things, and that is a very real danger. (See Q62 *'Should we explain if she appears rude to strangers?'*)

25. Why does he keep losing things?

Dr Attwood describes how the child with AS's needs what he calls an 'Executive Secretary'–a job, he says, which often falls to the child's mother. Children with AS can find the task of organising themselves and their possessions pretty much beyond them. As adults they may become quite exceptionally tidy, ordering their lives so that, for example, all books on their shelves are kept alphabetically by author, but as children it all seems too much for them, and they are surrounded by chaos. Homework is lost, items of clothing go missing, school books and equipment are not taken to school. The so-called Executive Secretary's role is to help provide some order to this, perhaps providing colour-coded files to keep different subject work in, checking the school bag for homework and notes and packing the necessary equipment for each day.

As with so much, understanding that the disorganisation is part of the condition can help to reduce the frustration of this to all parties, and helps everyone to concentrate on solutions rather than on criticism. These days with the reducing costs of palm top computers there is technology to help in this area. Having an electronic diary (that can be programmed by a parent if necessary) can provide the organisational skills that the individual needs. Being told what to do and when by the computer may also relieve some of the pressure on parents who might otherwise have to take on the role. Additionally, the individual may well respond more favourably to the computer than to a parent – after all, computers are far more consistent and 'black and white' than most people!

26. Why does he always behave badly when we go shopping?

To be honest, shopping doesn't tend to bring out the best in most children, so perhaps this can at least in part be put down to the 'child' part of a-child-with-Asperger-syndrome, and not the AS part. However, it's also worth bearing in mind that many people are paid a great deal of money to make shopping as stimulating, as eye-catching, as attention-grabbing as possible. We may largely filter out the clashing colours, the visual jokes, the music, the smells, the cold of the freezer aisles... but these may still be getting through to your son. If he behaves 'badly' when shopping, he is probably trying to tell you something. In the end it may be simplest to listen, and shop when he's not with you, or to use the Internet. Some battles just aren't worth fighting. In addition, if you choose the Internet shopping option, it may be a good idea to involve your son. Learning skills such as this can be hugely beneficial later on in life.

27. Why does she like watching the same thing over and over again on DVD?

The same thing on DVD stays the same thing. It is predictable, it always delivers the end you want and it doesn't depend on you to do it. Television, even more than the computer, is the ultimate non-participation activity. It can be trusted.

We are quick to see this as a problem - as the child wasting her time on a pointless, repetitive activity. It makes us uncomfortable.

When I have 'had enough' and feel I need a break I tend to lie in the bath, often re-reading an old book or magazine. I am a 'typically functioning adult', so no one tries to stop me. And I do, eventually, get out of the bath and return to my normal life.

If your child needs to watch the same thing over and over on television, I would not see that as a problem. I would have thought that the total time spent watching television, and therefore not interacting with anyone in any sort of social context, is more relevant.

If you decide that an hour's television after school is fair enough to help her to unwind, does it really matter if that hour is spent watching David Attenborough wildlife programmes, repeats of Mr Bean or the same old episode of The Simpsons? She probably knows what she needs best to relax and recharge before you tempt her back out into social interaction.

28. Why didn't she wish me Happy Birthday?

The simple answer to this is probably: because it didn't occur to her that she should. There are so many points of social etiquette like this; not answering the question "How do you do?" with a fully detailed run-down of your health, saying, "You look nice" and not "you've had your hair cut" when you notice someone has changed their hair, or, as an adult, remembering to tell your partner that you love him, even though you already told him last year. Tell your daughter next year that you would like her to wish you a happy birthday, or - better yet - prompt her to do it about other people's birthdays in the meantime. After a few reminders you may find that she says it spontaneously to you one year soon - and it will be worth so much more from her than it will be from anyone else!

29. Why does she like sleeping in a sleeping bag?

You get 'into' a sleeping bag in a way that you cannot do under a duvet and a sleeping bag wraps you up and gives you pressure from all sides. Some children with AS may find the light pressure of a duvet irritating or even painful, and prefer the tight, firm pressure of being wrapped into a sleeping bag, tightly tucked into a bed with sheets or weighted under a heavy quilt. Certainly it is worth experimenting with each of these, as anything which aids a peaceful night's sleep has got to be good for all parties. (*See 'Why doesn't he sleep much at night?' Q.* 22) If your daughter prefers a sleeping bag this is relatively easy to accommodate, and it has a real advantage for you: you can take it with you. Getting a child with AS to go to sleep in a strange bed can be a struggle which ruins any trip or holiday before you even get started. If your daughter is choosing to sleep in a sleeping bag already, you are off to a good start! It is sometimes a good idea, if your child has a favourite sleeping bag to buy more than one of the same make in case the original dies a death over time. While we may assume any sleeping bag is as good as the next one, the same may not be the perception of your child with AS!

30. Why is he frightened of stupid things?

It is only thought 'stupid' if someone is afraid of something of which we are not. A person with AS may well find different things alarming than other people do, and he may also be astonishingly 'brave' (i.e. un-alarmed by something which most people would find terrifying). Neither can be seen as a value judgement.

Fear is fear. Often it is useful. We all teach our children, for example, a healthy fear of crossing the road in order to keep them safe. Sometimes, though, with a child with AS the fear is misdirected. Our children may be frightened by literal interpretations of harmless things (for example, "turn left at the Red Lion" ...There's a LION??), or they may be overwhelmed by a sensory effect which we cannot perceive. They may be alarmed because they are unable to anticipate what is going to happen. Whatever the reason, the fear is real and should not be taken less seriously because we may not share it. Fear and anxiety are immensely common by-products of having to manage AS in a non-AS world, and we need to be alert constantly to, and constantly working to reduce, anxiety levels in our children. (See Q33 *'Why does he cover his ears when he's frightened?'*)

31. Why does she talk to strangers on the underground?

Children with AS may fail to modify their behaviour between dealing with friends and family and with total strangers. Thus your daughter may well inform the stranger sitting opposite on the underground that she is going to see the model of the Blue Whale at the Natural History Museum because it is a life-sized model of the biggest mammal that ever lived on this planet and there are still some in the seas today although no-one is sure how many and they are thought to be getting scarcer…Such an advance may astonish someone who is unaware of Asperger syndrome, but there is no intrinsic harm in it. Her approach is socially naïve, and can sometimes be misinterpreted (see *'Why does he say rude things?' Q. 24 and 'Should we explain if she appears rude to strangers?'* Q62). There are also other potential problems (*See 'How do we explain sexual dangers?'* Q61)). She is doing nothing wrong, but you may nevertheless decide to work with her on to whom to speak, where and when. She will need to get this 'right' as she grows up and begins to travel independently, if only for safety's sake.

32. Why does he have to spoil every big event?

The trouble with 'big events' is that they are out of the ordinary. People behave differently, routines change, the usual rules may be suspended. For a child with AS these may have an unsettling effect, and he may indicate this by 'behaving badly'. Just when you are focussing on something else, his autism comes to the fore. It can feel like it is unrelenting.

However, logically, it is hardly surprising. AS, as a condition, is there all the time, every day and it doesn't go away just because something else is happening. What may 'go away' are the supports which the person with AS has in place to help him, which is when the AS goes back to being unmanageable.

The solution is to deal with the AS first and then to plan the big event around that. There is no reason why your son with AS should spoil occasions, as long as his needs are still being met. Think about what you are expecting him to wear, to eat, to do and compare that with what he chooses. Will anyone really mind if he wears a t-shirt to the wedding, or reads quietly during the service? Your son with AS *is* different. Accepting that difference and accommodating it is the quickest way to minimising how different he seems – to others, and to himself. (*See 'Should we forget about Christmas?' Q. 97*)

33. Why does he cover his ears when he's frightened?

Shutting off the senses is a common phenomenon in all young children - not just those with AS - and indeed even in adults. If you are frightened, aren't you tempted to close your eyes? I think it is part of the "If I hide they won't find me" approach to fear management!

In a sense, the child with AS who covers his ears is being more efficient. Not hearing allows you still to see (and assess, and presumably run from) what alarms you, while minimising how much it frightens you. Next time you are watching a horror film, try it out for yourself. You can cover your eyes (or hide behind the cushion), but you are still frightened, and what's more, you miss the plot. Alternatively, try pressing the 'mute' button. Now you can see what is going on, but somehow it no longer seems so terrible.

Covering his ears may be a general sign that your son is vulnerable to aural overload. He may be shutting out the sound, and not actually be frightened at all. Whatever his reason, discomfort or fear, he is indicating distress, and, as in Q30 (*'Why is he frightened of stupid things?'*), whether you share that distress or not, it needs to be taken seriously.

34. Why isn't he brilliant at maths?

You may find that, as soon as you get the diagnosis, everyone assumes that your son will be a maths wizard. This can be depressing if he is, in fact, barely numerate. In fact, although many people with AS do undoubtedly have an aptitude for maths, there is nothing in the condition to say it is inevitable. Also, you may find that your son finds some calculations surprisingly easy, but finds 'real life' problems almost impossible. Certainly the "Ten elephants are in the jungle. Six go to the watering hole. How many are left?" - type of question is quite likely to cause problems. My son would be so outraged that this is against elephant behaviour (elephants, apparently, stay together and visit the waterhole as a group) that he would never get round to the maths.

As with so many aspects of your son's ability, his performance in maths may well be uneven. He may find apparently 'easy' things like learning times tables almost impossible, and he may have - to you - odd ways of working out calculations. As with most of the curriculum, you are likely to have more success if you let him, to an extent, take the lead. Just because a technique works for most children, doesn't mean it will work for him. He may not be able to do the work which is set, but that could be as much to do with how it is presented as to do with his innate ability. Be optimistic!

35. **Why does he go off by himself**?

Dr Tony Attwood has a famous 'cure' for autism: to go into a room by yourself and shut the door. There is, he says, no autism in solitude. If your difficulties lie in the social world it is hardly surprising that you need time by yourself, away from social demands, to relax and recover. As long as this solitude is by the choice of the person with autism (and not because he feels *unable* to be more social) then it should, I think, be respected. If going off by yourself makes you feel stronger and more able to face all the demands of the social world again then it is to be recommended. If only we could all minister to ourselves as effectively!

Section Two
What next: What can we do to help?

....

36. Why do we always have to make plans?

A child with AS may find it hard to switch from task to task. He may also have security in knowing what he is doing. He may have very little other control over his environment, where sights, sounds, smells assault him and people behave with infinitely unpredictable strangeness most of the time. His stress is likely to be greatly reduced if he knows what is happening. For example, if he knows he is going to watch television to the end of Scooby Doo, then he is going out or that you and he are going food shopping at the supermarket and then to the library, this is likely to give him a feeling of control or security. If he has had a hand in choosing these tasks, his security is likely to be even greater. Most of us need a calendar or diary to feel we have control over our lives. Providing a simple schedule for your child can act in the same way. With it you can plan what is to happen, agree it and as far as possible stick to that plan. It gives a nicely ordered feel, and is a small price to pay for making the world so much more hospitable for your child. Like so many things, you may find your child doesn't need it, but it is a technique which is worth a try. Try it, then ask him. In the end he will be the one to decide whether it helps him or not. (See also Q45 *'Why does our whole family seem to be ruled by the clock?'*)

37. Why were we told to get him a gym ball?

One of the seemingly more wacky techniques which may be useful in managing AS is that of applying deep pressure. Some children with AS have problems with sensory processing, and it may be that not enough messages get back to the child's brain for him to orientate himself. Your son may feel literally as if he is floating off into space. If he becomes jittery and sensory seeking (usually jumping, spinning or throwing himself around) it seems that deep pressure can be a tremendous relief. You could try squashing him under mats or pillows, or rolling him under a gym ball, gradually increasing the amount of weight and pressure. You may be able, almost, to see the steam coming out of his ears as he relaxes. Temple Grandin, who is a highly respected writer on the subject of autism, and who has autism herself, used the technique to design cattle-handling equipment. The technique can be incorporated into a 'sensory diet' which you find works best for your child. Jumping on the trampoline, balancing on a balance board, throwing and catching, tensing and relaxing muscles, swinging and spinning can all be practised to help your child develop his sensory processing ability. (See Q13 *'Why can't he sit still?'*)

38. Why buy her a trampoline?

One of the sensory processing problems often associated with AS is a need for the child to keep moving to orientate herself in space. Your daughter may crave the sensory feedback of jumping and balancing. Left to herself she would probably jump up and down on the sofa, or on the bed, no doubt breaking each and getting into plenty of trouble. The trampoline gives an outlet for this energy and allows her to give herself the sensory input she needs. It is also great fun, particularly when combined with catching, heading or hitting a ball. It is all excellent at helping her develop her sensory processing, and her interaction – and it keeps her out of trouble. Not bad for the price.

39. Should we give in to routines?

Although many children with AS do seem to have fairly rigid routines and habits, it is not clear whether these are intrinsic in the condition or more a result of anxiety, brought on by having to manage AS in a non-AS world. I think it is important to ask yourself what purpose each routine is serving before you decide whether to try to stop it. For example, does your son always walk the indirect path to the school door because he believes this keeps him safe? Or does he do it because he likes to see the way the light is reflected off the top window? Or does he do it because he's playing a game where the path is the runway of a spaceship? Or does he do it because he doesn't realise that the other path would get him to the same place? Or is it because it gets a response from you? Or because there was dog mess on the other path last time he looked? Or because… you name it! There will be a reason, even if it is not one which makes immediate sense to you. Our son once told us that he liked his new shoes because the left one didn't hurt. It hadn't occurred to him to tell us (or the shoe fitter) that the right one DID hurt. The AS world is just slightly different to ours. Trying to get insight into it through our children is a fascinating task.

40. Why take him to a Speech and Language Therapist?

Although it is not strictly speaking classified as a Speech and Language disorder, AS often manifests itself to the outside world as such. It is, after all, a condition which affects communication. Specialist Speech and Language therapists do much more than deal with 'speech impediments' such as stammers and lisps. Their interest in AS language development is in the child's use of social, semantic and pragmatic language. How does the child use language to communicate? How does the language use of a child with AS differ from that of a neuro-typical child? Does the child use language in a concrete, inflexible way? Does he bring a literal translation to metaphorical language? If you tell him that it is 'raining cats and dogs' does he literally expect feline and canine fall-out and if you tell him to 'pull his socks up' does he attend to the clothing on his feet?

Speech and Language specialists are also well placed to assess your son's level of language understanding. The verbosity of some children with AS can mask lack of understanding. Equally, some children's halting speech style and apparent slow answering of questions can hide great intelligence. Of all the outward visible signs of the neuro-developmental difference inside the child with AS, speech and language is probably the most profound. It is what your son *says* which makes you realise how differently he perceives the world.

If communication is the key, both to understanding your son's differences and to explaining the world's differences to your son, then speech and language are the most powerful tools which you have at your disposal. If you can find a Speech and Language specialist with a real interest in and understanding of the place of language in autism, then he or she may well become your son's most powerful ally in his managing of his AS. (See also Q12 *'Why does she sometimes appear to be deaf?'* Q11 *'Why does it take her so long to answer a questions?'* Q24 *'Why does he say rude things?'* Q23 *'Why does she talk in a funny voice?'*)

41. Why do we keep playing board games?

Board games are great. They have a faintly nostalgic charm from the days when families would assemble in front of the fire (as opposed to the television or computer) and complete complex jigsaw puzzles together or sing around the piano. Just playing a board game as a family gives your family self-image a boost!

Seriously, though, these things have a purpose. Board games have rules and these are overt, not implied. They can be read and referred to, and then everyone knows where they are. They enable everyone to play on an equal footing, and for everyone to have a turn at both winning and losing. Board games circumnavigate Asperger syndrome, and enable your child with AS to play along with your other children and with you. They teach turn taking, strategy, observation of others' actions… and they are fun. They break down age barriers, and allow interaction for everyone from Grandparents to your student daughter's new boyfriend. Who could ask for more?

42. Why write her notes?

Many children with AS are highly visual learners. Many will learn to read very quickly, and to retain facts that they have read far more readily than those they have only heard. In addition, what is said is then invisible, gone; what is written remains constant and can be referred to again.

Your child may well be more likely to remember something if it is written down. Many typically functioning adults are exactly the same and need to make notes in a diary if they are to remember meetings, names or numbers. Writing instructions or reminders down for your child, if that helps her, merely makes sense.

The written prompt is taken a step further in the Social Story technique developed by Carol Gray. These stories follow a prescribed format, and have been found by many to be extremely effective.

We found that persuading his teacher to pass our son a note saying "Please don't suck your jumper" worked instantly, when verbal reminders, reprimands, explanations and even punishments had not. Sometimes the solution is simple. It is for us who know our children to suggest them, and to hope that others are eventually willing to take them on. (See Q16 *'Why can't she follow instructions?'*)

43. What are 'angry cards'?

You may find that your child seems to explode into rage on occasion with apparently no warning. These 'melt-downs' are distressing to everyone (*See 'How can I stop him from lashing out?' Q. 44*)

The lack of warning that meltdown is imminent may be partly an inability in your child to read the signs that she is getting angry, and partly lack of ability to express that anger or frustration. Working with her, as discussed, on reading the signs that she is getting upset may help, but she still has to find a way of expressing that.

Angry cards are simply pieces of card, possibly with a drawing done by the child, which say "I Am Angry!" They are kept somewhere immediately accessible (for example stuck with a magnet on the fridge), and the deal is that if you are presented with this card (and your daughter has used the card rather than biting, kicking or otherwise expressing her anger), then it must be taken seriously and acted upon, and, most importantly, the reason for your daughter's anger must be listened to. If she finds that it works, and presenting it means that her little brother is taken away, or that she doesn't have to eat the broccoli after all, then she will probably soon get into the hang of it. Angry cards can be transferred to school use (as long as the school agree to honour them), and in time can be phased out in favour of using a verbal phrase. They are not a long-term solution, but are a pragmatic alternative to the violent explosion in the medium term.

44. How can I stop him from lashing out?

Managing anger can be a real problem for the person with AS (*See 'What are Angry Cards?' Q.43*) Angry cards, as already described, can offer a way of getting 'heard' to the person who feels too overwhelmed to be able to be articulate. However, even before using an Angry Card, that person has to be able to stop himself from lashing out.

'Stopping himself' may be the key here. You cannot stop him. You literally cannot be there all the time, close enough to intercept every punch or kick. He may find it extremely difficult to stop himself from a physical manifestation of his anger and frustration. Try to come up with an alternative which works for your son. Having a kind of 'padded cell' to which he could go to scream, punch, kick, swear and generally let off steam is probably the ideal, but not strictly practical in most circumstances! An alternative could be a punch bag or cushions available to be hit, paper which can be torn and shredded. One of the most effective which I have seen was shown by a boy who, rather than punching or kicking, pushed against the wall as if he were trying literally to push the building over. This is good because walls are almost always available (trees could substitute in the outdoors), and perhaps more importantly the amount of effort is reflected by the amount of pressure. You can literally push as hard as you can, and get all that sensory feedback into your own body without any danger of either hurting yourself or of actually pushing the wall over. Try it yourself. It really is curiously satisfying!

Encourage your son to use this as an instant 'vent your frustration' safety valve, and then to use a technique such as Angry Cards to get the problem heard and sorted out. Whenever your son uses this technique it is imperative that a) it works and that you do your best to remove the source of the frustration and that b) he is rewarded for using it. If he is going to do this at school, make sure that NO-ONE is going to tell him off or make him stop. If he is to trust you, then you must make sure that this alternative to lashing out is respected.

45. Why does our whole family seem to be ruled by the clock?

Having a timetable to the day, like having a visual schedule (*See Why do we always have to make plans?' Q.36*), is a way of giving the day overt order for the child with AS. Whereas your neuro-typical children may moan about, but essentially cope with, the need to stop playing and be taken to the supermarket, or your sudden appearance to turn off the television and demand that they go out and get some fresh air, or your remembering just as they sit down at the computer that they haven't done their homework… your child with AS is likely to find each a strain. Planning the day and indicating when and for how long an activity should be helps to give a reassuring structure to the day. Events which used to trigger melt down in your AS child (bath time, bed time, sitting down to meals), may be no problem at all if the child knows that they are coming. Use of a five-minute warning before a change of activity does wonders too (differing durations of egg timers can be a Godsend), as does giving a choice. "You can either turn off the computer straight away, or play for five more minutes and then turn if off with a happy face" may not really be much of a choice, but it can make a difference to your child.

46. What should I tell her to do if she gets lost?

One of the more alarming traits of AS in young children is their apparent lack of fear of getting lost. Most children (and indeed most creatures in the animal kingdom) stay instinctively close to their parents and become distressed if separated from them. Our children seem to lack this basic self-preservation instinct. Ours would, sadly, be the isolated baby lamb picked off by the wolf pack or the penguin chicks freezing alone in the cold. They wander off to look at what interests them and it is for us to try to keep up. The 'invisible rubber band' which normally connects child to parent seems to be broken.

Because of this it is perhaps even more important for children with AS than for most children to have a strategy in place should they find themselves 'lost'. The old advice to find a policeman is really not of much use. What we have found which seems to work well is the advice to "Find a woman with a child younger than you, and say, 'Please help me, I have lost my Mum" (Initially we said, "Find a woman with a pushchair", but the only time our son did get lost was in a supermarket, and all the mothers seemed to have their children in the trolleys!) This is quite specific advice, which should allow her to target someone who is likely to help her (and who is less likely to harm her), and give her the phrase to use. The alternative is to say to go to the people on the tills, but this only works in shops. In addition, as the child gets older it may be necessary to supplement the advice with a card which indicated that your daughter has AS, together with your mobile number so you can be contacted. The National Autistic Society provide cards which can be carried which give a simple explanation of AS to help avoid confusion or the accusation that your daughter's manner means that she is being rude. Alternatively you may want to make your own, with your daughter's input, which she can use should this situation arise.

47. Should we insist, even if she gets upset?

Part of being a parent is being prepared to do things which our children don't like. From the time you held your newborn baby's foot out for the 'heel-prick' blood-test, even though you knew it would make her cry, you have been prepared to do some things, sometimes, for other reasons than to make your daughter immediately happy. Hard though it is, we sometimes have to take the grief because we believe that overall what we are doing is for a greater good.

Much of our time as parents of a child with AS is spent trying to stop that child from getting upset. 'Melt-downs' are distressing for all, and are a sign that something is wrong in your child's world or in the way they can communicate about it. 'Meltdowns' are those particularly autistic types of distress when your child has gone beyond upset, beyond angry…beyond reason. We work (hard, often!) at understanding and then avoiding the triggers for these.

There are, however, perfectly normal periods of 'upset' for a child with AS, just as for any other child. You would not be doing your child a favour if at the first sign of a down-turned mouth you gave in to what she wanted. Give her ways of communicating why she wants/doesn't want something, give her warnings and schedules so that she can prepare for things she doesn't like, and be prepared to listen when she REALLY doesn't want to do something… but beyond that, stick to your guns about the normal stuff. Your daughter needs to learn the same lessons as any other child: that sometimes we all have to do things which are boring, or which aren't our first choice, or have to stop doing what we enjoy. The tricky part with a child with AS is to differentiate between a child's natural disinclination to - for example - go shopping, and a real sensory distress at going shopping, or between her reluctance to turn off the computer and her lack of understanding that she had to turn it off. Give her more chance than you would most children to 'put her case', in order to compensate for communication difficulties, then stick to your instincts. It's not a parent's job to be popular!

48. Is it okay to keep on holding his hand?

Like Q 58 (*'Should we let her do the same things as other kids her age?'*), this is to do with behaviour which is appropriate to your child's development, as opposed to his actual age. A parent holds onto the hand of a young child to stop him from getting lost, and to ensure he doesn't get into danger, for example by darting into the road. It is not much comfort to you that you weren't "making him look like a baby" if your child has no road sense and gets hit by a ten-ton truck.

On the other hand, your child's social antennae are weak, and where neuro-typical children become aware of the opinions of their peers and wriggle away from holding your hand - as part of the whole necessary process of moving away from you as parent in a wider sense - at a prescribed age, the child with AS may not be aware of this peer pressure. It is for you to try, as far as is possible, to protect him from 'looking ridiculous'. It will not help him to be seen holding hands with his mum at age 12 and, while this is a minor consideration when put against being hit by a truck, it is nevertheless a consideration. If you really do not trust him around roads at an age when hand-holding is inappropriate, try to be devious. You could, for example, get him to help carry the shopping by holding onto the other handle of the bag. If nothing else, get him to walk on the inside, away-from-the-road side of the pavement - and do some work on 'road rules'. Ultimately you will not only not be there to hold his hand. You will not be there at all and road sense, like so much, is an essential skill to master.

49. How can we help him make friends?

Friendships, by definition, are social and AS is a condition which carries inherent social difficulties. You could even say that if people with AS could make friends easily (and keep them), the condition would be 'solved'. For the purposes of this question, a friend could be defined as someone with whom you have an equal relationship, who cares about you and about whom you care, and who compensates for your weaknesses just as you compensate for his/hers.

Undoubtedly, the complexities of this are a strain for the person with AS. Parents can feed appropriately aged children-of-their-friends into the child with AS's life, but real friendship is more than that. It may be tempting to find another child with AS in the hope that having this in common will prompt friendship. Sadly, all too often this just ends up with twice the degree of social interaction difficulties, made worse by competition for who is the cleverest or knows the most facts about dinosaurs (see

Q.50 *'Should we find him friends with AS?'*). The answer is not really this easy.

One answer, perhaps, is to stand back and take a look at what makes friendship at other stages of life. Past school age, the insistence that a friend be exactly your age dwindles away, as, to an extent, does the insistence that they be the same gender. Adult friendships can bridge age, gender, distance, life experience and culture - yet these are not what we immediately look for when wanting our AS child to have a 'friend'. We want him to have a friend of his age, with whom he can play the same as the other kids do. In other words, we want him to be 'normal'. We may have missed the point.

This is not to undermine the child with AS's intense desire to make friends. Just because someone lacks social skill does not mean that he does not crave friendship and acceptance just like everyone else, and one of the principal dangers of having AS is that of loneliness. If you are friendless you are also isolated, and more vulnerable to the playground 'predators'. Friendships serve many purposes.

In helping a child with AS navigate this whole difficult issue, it may help to analyse these different purposes served by friendships, and to try to give support to each separately. For example, you may decide that one element is that a friend is someone you walk to school with, possibly as much for safety as for companionship. You may have to look around for a parent who needs some help here, perhaps because she has to leave early for work and is struggling to get her child to school.

Perhaps she could drop her child off with you, both children could have an extra ten minutes together on the computer and then you could drive them both to school, dropping them just before the gate. This won't make the two children friends, but if managed well it may give at least an approximation of one element of it. Similarly, if a friend is someone who shares your interests, persuading the school to run lunchtime clubs around your son's special interest will give him access to people who speak his language and - perhaps as important - give him a safe haven to go to. A lot of this is about providing the practical benefits which friends naturally give, even if the friendships themselves are not developing.

For real friendship I would suggest giving your son access to people outside his immediate age range. Older children and adults, by being more socially mature themselves, can often bridge the gap in social aptitude. Similarly, allow your son to learn to express kindness and care for a friend by letting him play with or teach a much younger child. Both of these require an element of supervision.

Ultimately, parents can never find friends for their children. Friends, and lovers, are the people we find for ourselves as we grow away from dependence on our parents. Much of our self-image is reflected in our friends' value of us, and that has to be achieved for ourselves. As parents, all we can do is try to plug the danger gaps left by the absence of friends and to provide as many opportunities as possible for our child to maintain self-esteem. After all, if your son remains confident about being who he is (see Q85 *'Will he ever have a girlfriend?'*), there is no reason why his friendships won't develop naturally in time.

50. Should we find him friends with Asperger syndrome?

As already touched on in Q 49 (*'How can we help him make friends?'*), this is not the easy answer to friendship which it appears to be at first glance. Two children with AS have double the lack of tact and social skill. You may find you have twice the problem (although conversely two individuals who are not bothered by social faux pas with one another can get along extremely well.)

As your son gets older you may find that someone who *shares his intensity of interest* may make an ideal friend. In other words, the friendship is not based on the fact of their shared 'disability', but on the fact that - at last! - here is someone who cares about robotic inventions as much as your son. You may find that the two of them will be very happy, and companiable, researching their interest together. They may not, actually, interact all that much with each other, which brings you to a rich source of interaction for the older child with AS: the internet. Here it is possible to find all sorts of people who share the same interests, often to the same intensity, and who make very little personal demand on each other. The child with AS born this century is so much luckier, in this, than any of his predecessors. The internet could have been invented as his ideal communication tool!

A word of caution: you do need to monitor your son's use of the Net and make sure he is absolutely clear about internet safety rules.

As with all forms of communication, his naivety makes him vulnerable. That aside, it may be necessary to impose some rules to make sure that you allow time for you son to continue to practice his interaction skills out in the real world. The internet may largely by-pass AS problems, but it does nothing to help the person to overcome them. He needs real interaction with real people - often - if he is to hope to develop his skills. (See also Q52 *'How much computer time should we allow?'*)

51. Should we go along with his current 'Special Interest'?

Like the mother mentioned in Q 64 (*'How do we deal with obsessions?'*), you would, in a way, be daft not to. By rolling with your son's special interest you have won half the battle, in that you have his attention. As mentioned in Q3 (*'Why does he go on and on about things?'*), though, you do want to ease him forward into more than going on about what *he* knows. Try to accept his interest, and then use it to build and stretch. For example, if his interest is robots, why not design a robot together which would do the job of washing a car? Wash the car together first in order to work out the jobs – then take a trip to a car wash to see how the robotic car wash does it. You can take this further. If you ask, all sorts of unusual doors may open to you. If you write to one of the big car manufacturers, for example, and tell them that your son has AS and his special interest is robots, they may well allow you to visit and watch the automated factory machines at work. Use the advantage of your son's difference; clearly they can't let all kids in, but an exception is often allowed where others would not be. This is building real education and real experiences onto what already interests your son. He *is* special; he *does* know more about robots than most children of his age. By going along with this and building on it you are emphasising the positive aspects of AS, and building up your son's all-important self-esteem. And don't forget, a current special interest is likely to be the single biggest motivator for your child, so use this fact wisely!

52. How much computer time should we allow?

The short answer to this is probably, 'less than he would wish'! Computers hold an overwhelming attraction for many, indeed probably most, children with AS. They are predictable, the child is in charge, they don't make irrelevant social demands ...and they are fun!

Left on his own with a computer and a range of really good educational CD Roms, it is quite possible that your son would educate himself. Teaching through the computer ('asocial' learning) is usually a great deal better suited to the child with AS than teaching through a classroom.

The problem, as already touched upon in Q 50 (*'Should we find him friends with AS?'*), is that although the computer may play to your son's strengths, it does little to help with his weaknesses. He does not learn many social skills through the computer. That said, it does allow him to play successfully with virtually any child who visits the house who knows how to operate the same two-player game, and it does give him a spurious 'street cred' when he is the only child who can reach level 31!

Personally I feel that denying a child with AS access to the computer is to take away a medium tailor-made for him, and is to deny him access to something at which he shines and on which he is happy. All children need to be limited in their time playing computer games, otherwise they might never eat, sleep or leave the house. A child with AS is the same, just more so.

53. Which sports should we encourage him to play?

Team sports may be a bit of an anathema to a child with AS. He may grasp fully the need to get the football between the posts, but the subtlety of the build-up may pass him by. It's possible he may make an excellent (if somewhat selfish) striker, or that he is good in goal. Or it may be that team sports are a disaster, in which case try to protect him from them as far as possible.

One-against-one non-contact sports are more likely to be a success for a child with AS. There is nothing in tennis or badminton, for example, which is likely to cause problems. The rules are explicit and no interaction is required. However, the social life around the game (which is the reason many people play) is still likely to cause difficulty. His physical and co-ordination immaturity may also make racquet games difficult.

The most likely successful sport for the individual with AS is one where he is essentially competing against himself. Running, for example, is essentially solitary. On the other hand your son may see all sport as essentially pointless. It may be a struggle for you to encourage activity to maintain fitness, especially if your son is a computer game enthusiast. Something like orienteering, which has an element of problem solving, might work, as might a sport such as judo or taekwondo which has an element of formality together with the potential to build self-esteem. It may be a matter of trying a number of different sports, and being prepared to move on - perhaps many times as he grows up - as each throws up its problems.

54. How do I prepare her for puberty?

Puberty is a disruptive, tempestuous time in anybody's life, and perhaps particularly in that of someone with AS. Bodies change, feelings and desires run riot, and the social rules become highly confusing.

It is important to prepare the adolescent with AS in plenty of time for the physical changes of puberty. There is no reason why she shouldn't have a complete and informed grasp of the facts of puberty. Body changes, pubic hair growth and menstruation are all fully manageable in a scientific, factual context, and young people with AS are likely to view these changes perhaps more dispassionately than their neuro-typical peers. (Please note that this applies to most children with AS - however there are a small number for whom the distress caused to them by knowing that something will be happening to them but not knowing *when* actually outweighs the stress of puberty itself).

Sexual feeling, self-image and attractiveness, mood swings and confusion are not so easily dealt with. This is a stormy period in most people's lives, and young people with AS are likely to be more vulnerable than most, largely due to lack of social or peer support. Puberty is about change – from child to adult – and change is not something which is always easy for people with AS. I think, as well as preparing her, you need to prepare yourself; it may be a bumpy ride! (See also Q98 *'Will he get better?'*)

55. What happens if we have to move house?

Moving house is a major disruption for all concerned, but perhaps especially for someone who has Asperger syndrome. The loss of security and familiarity can be hard, and the person may not recognise a new house as 'home'.

Preparation is the key. Tell your child as soon as you are sure where you are moving to (but not too early – make sure that you have the house first, otherwise you will have to deal with further insecurity and loss if that sale falls through) and keep telling him what may seem obvious to you, in other words that he is moving too, as is the sofa, the computer, teddy, his little sister, you… You may find that you need to reassure him about many things ("yes, we are taking the tin opener"), and have to deal with grief about leaving what cannot be taken ("no, we are leaving this bath, but there is another bath in the new house.") Take pictures of the new house, and draw plans to show him where the furniture, computer, television and so on will be. It may be helpful to spend considerable time on his bedroom, agreeing what colour it will be painted (the same colour as his current room, perhaps), and making sure that his bed, his chest of drawers, his lampshade all move straight across, and are positioned in the same place relative to each other. This is not a good time to upgrade his furniture and get him a new big-boy bed.

Packing can be traumatic in itself. Although most of us use packing up a house as a chance to have a good clear-out, this is likely to cause distress to a child with AS, who is already feeling the strain. It's okay to pack EVERYTHING from his room – broken toys, games with the bits lost, freebies from junk-food restaurants and all. If your son knows that ALL his toys and possessions will be in the new house, he is likely to be reassured. It can be a good idea to pack up and move out much of his 'stuff' from his room, gradually, as the move approaches, so that on the day he just has his bed, his furniture, his curtains and one box of toys and books. All these can be moved and unpacked on the day, so that the new room is immediately a close approximation of the old. I would suggest making up the bed in the new house with the bedding taken straight off the old bed (rather than with clean bedding), and similarly letting him sleep in the same pyjamas. As humans we can discount the reassuring effect of our own smell.

Moving house is a major upheaval, but sometimes it can't be helped. Keep reassuring your child, and be prepared for a setback in anxiety-based behaviour. This can be a time for the strategic use of the computer. If you buy him his absolutely most-wanted computer game just before the move and let him have free access to using it, and then make sure the computer is the first thing to be working in the new house and again let him get on with it, he may almost not notice the change of venue!

56. Should we change our diet?

Many children with AS are already fanatically cautious eaters. Getting a balanced diet into them can be a monumental battle in its own right, and it is not surprising that parents already facing this challenge should quail when advised by some well-meaning acquaintance that a strict avoidance diet is needed. It may be more than they can bear.

If it is, relax and wait until you're ready. Trying different diet combinations (most usually eliminating dairy products - casein - and gluten) is an increasingly common approach, and a great many parents believe it makes a difference. Medical science is lagging behind, but some indications are starting to trickle through that there is a sound scientific basis for this. Some links to check out the science of this are provided at the back of this book.

However, removing these elements from your child's diet may not be easy. For a start, your child may be totally hooked, and suffer withdrawal symptoms when deprived of his 'fix'. Children denied gluten in their diet have been known to chew carpet tiles to satisfy their cravings. The diet is also complicated (it takes a while to navigate your way around the ingredients) and can be expensive. In addition it provides a further barrier to social inclusion. The sharing of a meal is a fundamental piece of social glue; not being able to accept that slice of birthday cake can make your child even further excluded.

Probably the time will come when you will decide to try experimenting with diet as a way to manage your child's symptoms. It is certainly an avenue worth exploring - but don't let yourself be bullied into it until you're ready. It is an added strain at a time when you're only just coming to terms with the implication of your child's diagnosis. You can be made to feel like a bad parent if you don't immediately embrace a whole different way of eating for your whole family, and this 'blame culture' is not helpful. Remember, none of this is a matter of 'fault'.

57. What about vitamins?

It is hugely tempting to try to find a pill to cure the problem. There is also a growing market 'out there' aiming to persuade you that this decontaminant or this mineral supplement will make all the difference. It is very hard to resist these pressures. After all, what if they are right?

One thing is certain and that is that no one can follow all the advice that is around about autism. For one thing, much of it is contradictory. Some of it is based on sound scientific research and some, to be frank, is not. I think it is for each individual family to pick their own way through this minefield. I give some contact details at the back of this book, although this is by no means exhaustive. 'Exhausting' might be nearer the mark! My advice would be to pace yourself as you decide what treatments, supplements or programmes you are going to try with your child. Some may well be of benefit, but none is a cure. Sometimes it is easier to immerse yourself in trying to find solutions than it is to get on with enjoying life with your child, as he is. In our family, we take some of the supplements, follow some of the diets, have taken some of the 'programmes'. At the moment our son is happy and confident – and I can't say whether that is due to him, the pills, or us but we're just delighted he is doing so well. Take the pills with a pinch of salt – and good luck!

58. Should we let her do the same things as other kids her age?

As a society, we are obsessed with age. The world is full of things you 'should' do at certain ages, regardless of your own personal development. You 'should' be able to do joined-up writing at age 7, be able to walk to school by yourself at age 11, have had your first kiss by age 14… Your daughter is likely to hit these various milestones later than her peers. Part of the social isolation of AS is this social immaturity, where the child has only just learned how to join in 'run about' games and suddenly everyone is into standing around chatting. Your daughter is likely to be always struggling to catch up, and this can be painful to watch.

It is most likely that it will not be a good idea to let your daughter do things which other children of her age do. They may be mature enough to walk to school alone at eleven, for example, but your daughter may simply not have the skills to do so safely at that age. She may be unable to judge the speed of cars, may not have the flexibility to cross to the other side of the road if there is a hazard such as road-works, may not be able to cope with a dog which approaches her. She is unlikely to have the social understanding to cope should she meet someone – child or adult – who wishes her harm in some way, and is unlikely to have the resources to gain help if she needs it. She may be many years older than her peers before these skills are acquired, and until then you are not being over protective if you provide assistance while she needs it. A child with AS may be intellectually very advanced, may be physically no different to those around her, but she is hugely vulnerable. As her parent it may well fall to you to protect her when others see no need. You may well have to take some flak about 'over-protectiveness'. Don't let it bother you!

59. Should I teach him to swim?

All children should probably be taught to swim, purely on safety grounds. In the case of a child with AS this may be particularly important if his awareness of danger is poor, and if his sensory seeking makes him more likely to want to throw himself into ponds. Our son used to love jumping into deep water long before he could swim (terrifying!). Conventional swimming lessons are not always of much use, since they tend to concentrate on water confidence and on stroke technique rather than on drowning-prevention in our 'unusual' children. You may also find that your son finds swimming classes noisy and disorientating. Most pools offer 1:1 alternatives to classes, although if these take place during public swimming sessions there may well still be too much noise and distraction. Talk to your pool manager, who should have a 'disability policy' in place and who may be able to accommodate your son at quieter times. Sometimes the self-taught approach is best - you may find that your son will observe others in the pool, - and when he is ready take the plunge himself. However you eventually manage it, it really is important that you find a way to teach him to at least get to the surface to breathe.

60. What should we do if she's bullied at school?

The answer to this is: take it very seriously indeed. Children with AS are particularly vulnerable to – and unfortunately likely to be targeted by – bullying. Their social immaturity and isolation leaves them open to what Tony Attwood calls 'The Predators', and their communication differences may make them unable to, or unaware even that they can, report bullying to you.

Every school has an anti-bullying policy. It is advisable to familiarise yourself with it thoroughly even before a problem occurs. Keep communication with the school open and keep checking, with them and with her, where she sits in lessons, whom she works with, where she is at break-times, whom she is with, what she does. Bullying can be active (either physical attacks or verbal taunts) or passive (leaving out and isolation). It takes a committed and confident staff to deal with it, and it is difficult and time consuming. On the other hand, dealing with bullying is essential for the well being of all children in a school, and your vigilance and tenacity over your daughter's welfare may in the end have a benefit to all children.

Ultimately, if your best efforts do not stop the bullying, you may have to ask yourself whether it is fair to continue to compel your daughter to go into an environment which is unsafe. At the end of the day, she does not have to go to that school, or to any school (see Q 89 *'Does she have to go to school?'*). It is your job to keep her safe, and if you cannot do that when she is in that school environment, take her out. Her self-esteem and mental well-being are more important than mere convention. Depression and even suicidal thoughts are frighteningly prevalent in young people with AS. The matter needs taking very seriously indeed.

61. How do we explain sexual dangers?

So called 'Stranger Danger', an awareness that a stranger may be acting in a friendly way towards you because he wishes to do you harm, is a very difficult subject to broach with a young child with AS. On the whole I favour giving practical rules ("Do not leave the school grounds unless you are with me, your father or a teacher") rather than trying to explain the reasons behind the rules to the younger child with AS, who may otherwise become unduly anxious about the most innocent of approaches.

However, young people with AS are particularly vulnerable to sexual abuse, and the subject has to be tackled effectively to give protection. Again, one approach is a very practical one, for example agreeing which parts of the body may be touched, when and by whom, and what to do if someone else tries to do so. These rules need to be constantly - and realistically - updated as the child grows up, and parents may find that they are not the best people to handle this subject. A health worker, support teacher, family member or other well-placed adult may be better able to take on the role, but it is essential to make sure that SOME-ONE is there to help the young person with AS handle these, and all sexual matters. If everyone assumes that 'someone else will do it', young people with AS are frighteningly vulnerable.

62. Should we explain if she appears rude to strangers?

This will vary tremendously from occasion to occasion. Sometimes, if trouble is escalating out of hand, explaining that your daughter has AS - or has autism, which more people have heard of - can stop an irate stranger in his tracks. Sometimes it is the only way to diffuse a situation.

On the other hand, it is important not to use the diagnosis as a 'get out'. You are not doing your daughter any favours if you give the impression that having AS is an excuse. Having AS may explain why she behaves as she does, and may make it harder for her to behave as others do, but it is not an excuse not to learn social rules. For example, she may not recognise that there is a queue at the library. If she pushes in and someone shouts at her, informing the stranger that she has AS may prevent the damage of being attacked for doing something your daughter did not realise was wrong. However, now that she does realise there is a queue, she will need to join it. Help her with this, teach her how to manage queuing - don't use her diagnosis as a free pass to get your books stamped more quickly! (See Q24 *'Why does she say rude things?'*)

63. How do we get him to the dentist?

...with difficulty! Visits to the dentist, to have new shoes fitted, to the hairdresser (see Q15 *'Why does he hate having his hair cut?'*) can be a real problem for the child with AS.

Preparation and desensitisation can both help. Talk your child through what a dentist does. Get some books on teeth and oral care. Let your child (if he wants to) have a good look around inside your mouth. Talk to him about what a dentist does and why. If possible, visit the dentist and let your child set the pace. He may just want to look round. He may be willing to sit in the chair. He may let the dentist put the smooth mirror in his mouth and have a look around… Most dentists are becoming much better at dealing with a whole range of people who find them frightening. Tell your dentist in advance that your child has AS. If he does not allow plenty of time and caution in his approach, then it is probably worth changing your dentist. Remember that the law is on your side here. A dentist should 'make reasonable adjustments' to accommodate your child so make sure the practice is aware of what your child's needs are (e.g. not having to wait in the busy waiting room) with plenty of advance warning.

64. How do we deal with obsessions?

There are broadly two different types of obsessions. One type is a Special Interest which dominates the person's life, to the potential detriment of other interests. The other is anxiety behaviour, such as constant hand washing, or the need to turn off all the electrical sockets before leaving the house. They are different, and have different causes.

Special Interests seem to be a feature of most people with AS's lives. The person develops an interest, and wants to spend more time on this, to know more about it, to read about it, memorise facts about it, live it to an extent which is outside what could be considered usual, and to an extent which some might consider obsessive. Sometimes we find ourselves, even unwittingly, encouraging this. "How do I stop my son's obsession with Thomas the Tank Engine?" asks the mother, holding the hand of a little boy wearing Thomas shirt, hat, socks and shoes, holing a Thomas toy, reading a Thomas book and who sleeps in Thomas pyjamas under a Thomas duvet! There is a contradiction here: the mother is worried that her son's interest is becoming obsessive, yet she knows how much pleasure it gives him and so buys him the gifts. She already knows that the way to get his interest and interaction is to use his interest. She knows that he is far more likely to learn to count if he is counting trucks which need to be taken to the branch-line, and far more likely to sit at table if his food is on a Thomas plate. What she worries about, perhaps, is that this is it: for the rest of his life her son is going to be wearing Thomas the Tank engine socks! In fact, this is unlikely. Experience shows that it is the intensity of the interest that remains constant in AS, not the subject itself. Her son's interest is likely to shift (perhaps to dinosaurs or planets), and then shift again. Ultimately, he will become interested in a subject which may well become the centre of his studies and indeed his career. The single-mindedness of the person with AS is unusual, and can be wearing for the rest of the family in its various manifestations, but is not, in itself, necessarily a bad thing. In fact, for some individuals this side of AS is exactly what will lead to a good job in the longer term. (See Q51 *'Should we go along with his current special interest?'*).

More worrying are the obsessions to do with anxiety. These can seriously interfere with the person's life. If the person feels he has to wash his hands for a full minute before touching food, this can increase to five minute, ten minutes, twenty. Or he may feel he has to wash his hands, dry them, then wash them again ...and again. It is important to address the anxiety in this type of situation, not target the action itself. If the person really believes that he is protected by this degree of hand washing, it is verging on the inhuman to lock the bathroom door and prevent access. Although this type of behaviour, and this level of anxiety, are prevalent in people with AS, there is nothing in the condition itself which means it is inevitable. Work with the person with AS's stress levels, look at his environment, both sensory and social, find out just how intolerable various parts of his day may be - and do something to change them. This sort of obsessive behaviour is a sign of distress. The last thing the person needs is his routines (which may be the only thing allowing him to cope) being targeted.

65. How do I stop him from getting into trouble?

Undoubtedly, one of the advantages of disclosure is that it can prevent a child with AS from getting into trouble for something which he didn't intend to be rude, rebellious or disrespectful. (See Q62 *'Should we explain if she appears rude to strangers?'*) Once teachers are aware of AS in your child, and always supposing that they have had sufficient training and support (not always a safe supposition to make, admittedly), behaviour which is inappropriate should be met with a model of how to be more appropriate, rather than a reaction to what was initially said or done. Equally, in the wider community a greater understanding of AS could result in fewer people with AS getting "into trouble" with authority or the law.

Your son's social naivety may also lead him into trouble. He is vulnerable to those who would use him, who would in effect 'set him up' to break the law. People he may see as friends, for example, may try to use him as a front for crime in just the same way as children at school may be tempted to set him up to say or do inappropriate things in class. In school, the teachers' awareness of AS and its vulnerabilities should help enormously. In the wider world, you may have to continue to rely on your vigilance and be prepared to explain about AS as and when difficulties arise.

66. How do I get him to understand about personal space?

A child with AS may not understand that we have really quite specific, although usually unspoken, rules about how close we get to another person. A mother may hug a child, a close friend may ruffle a child's hair, an acquaintance may offer to shake hands. Getting personal space wrong is one of the aspects of AS which seems to most bother those without AS. Someone you don't know that well standing too close to you, perhaps reaching out and touching you can be immensely threatening to some people.

Try drawing a set of concentric circles for your son. Put his name or picture in the middle, and then add people in ever widening circles out from that. You might put parents and siblings in the first circle out from the middle, other family members in the next, friends and teachers in the next and so on, out to, perhaps, the postman in the outermost circle.

You then need some large sheets of paper, or the sort of yard or patio which you can draw on in chalk. Draw rings, showing that actual distance correlates to the distance of the rings on the paper. Parents are in the rings closest to the child and the child can reach out and touch them without difficulty. The teacher at school is in a further circle, so your son should try to stand at that slightly further distance. The postman may never get close enough to be able to do more than get a wave or a shouted hello!

Of course your son, being clever, will soon spot that this doesn't really work. Teachers move close to pupils when they are viewing their work; everyone is put on an inner-circle-of-family footing when you travel on a crowded train. You are going to have to use these as starting points for further work. Human beings are not simple, and do not obey simple rules - which is why the task facing the person with AS trying to make sense of it all is so difficult, and why we need to keep on helping as much as we can.

67. Should I let her wear whatever she wants?

Some children with AS are very particular about what they wear, not through a fashion sense but because of a need for comfort. It may drive you insane that she will, if allowed, wear the same t-shirt day after day after day, but there may be a very good reason for it. The labels in the back of some clothes, for example, can scratch some children so badly that it in intolerable. Other children cannot stand restriction around their waists and will only wear clothes with loose elastic. Others cannot stand the feeling of socks, particularly the ridge at the toe where they are sewn together (though thankfully these days you can buy socks with the ridge on the outside).

Some of this can be overcome with detective work and a bit of flexibility. For examples, socks worn inside out may be more comfortable. On the whole, though, I would go with pragmatism and reckon this is another of those fights which aren't worth getting involved in. If your daughter likes one particular t-shirt, buy her ten identical and let her get on with it. You may have some arguments ahead at school, but in my opinion these are arguments you should be able to win. Any school worth its good name should surely be more interested in facilitating a good personal learning environment for your daughter than on insisting on one particular brand of shirt, even though it may take them a little persuasion to see it that way. Good luck! (See also Q 92 *'Doesn't he care what he looks like?'*)

68. What about the dangers of drink and drugs?

In one way your child with AS may actually have an early advantage in avoiding the dangers of alcohol and drug abuse. The strongest element in the starting of these is often peer pressure, and this may be weaker for the child with AS. In addition, campaigns telling of the health dangers of drink and drugs are likely to work well and be a strong influence on the child with AS, as are already adhered-to rules. If your child is on a gluten-free diet, for example, he may refuse any substance he is offered on those grounds alone.

However, it would be naïve to be complacent. Many people use alcohol and recreational drugs because they feel it helps them be at ease in social contexts, and this is precisely the place where the person with AS struggles most. If he feels that a drink or two makes him able to interact more successfully, he is very likely to become dependent - socially if not yet physiologically. Both drink and drugs can be used to repress social inhibitions, and as such they may seem very attractive to the person with AS. He is also vulnerable to the person who 'befriends' him in order to get him drunk, or to get him to carry or supply drugs. People with AS do not have a strong antennae to detect when they are being used.

Drink and drugs awareness education is a good start to helping the person with AS manage this danger, but vigilance remains most important. As in Q58 (*'Should I let her do the same things as other kids her age?'*), the person with AS may require an element of supervision for much longer than his neuro-typical peers. AS makes people vulnerable to all sorts of abuse. There is nothing wrong with protecting them, even into adulthood.

69. How can I encourage personal hygiene?

Personal hygiene may become an issue if a person with AS sees no reason to wash/change clothing/use deodorant, and does not have sufficient social skills to be aware when others find this offensive. Einstein was reputed to have huge problems in this area. As with being 'rude' (Q 24 *'Why does he say rude things?'*), this is initially a problem for the people around the person with AS, rather than a problem directly for the person with AS himself.

However, to get on with people in an every day context, it is a tremendous help if you do not smell and do not have food crusted down the front of your shirt. The simplest approach to overcoming this problem is probably to be very practical. Set rules, for example that a bath or shower must be taken at least every other day, that teeth must be cleaned night and morning, that hair must be washed, clothing changed, deodorant applied and so on. The person with AS may find these matters irrelevant, but you can explain that that is what they are: rules for independent living, and all people (more or less) abide by them. Also, remember that many people with AS actually like routines - if you can include basic personal hygiene into a routine it is likely to become less of a problem. Sometimes, the ways to help a person with AS are entirely practical. If you can get him to present a socially acceptable face to the world, you are in fact helping him take huge strides in facilitating his social interaction. These are, supposedly, the things only your best friend would tell you. Be your son's 'best friend'!

Section Three

....

What about the rest of us? Living with AS in the family

70. Does that mean he'll never love us?

One of the tragedies of autism is the appearance that the child does not feel, nor crave, affection. It is very, very hard when your child wriggles out of a hug, pushes you away, shrugs off a kiss, screams when you try to hold him. The emotional effect on the parents is incalculable; it is quite frankly devastating.

You may find that you have to find other ways to show emotion. The character in 'The Curious Incident of the Dog in the Night-time' uses a palm-to-palm gesture to replace an embrace, and you may find your own versions of this which your son prefers.

The rejection of physical gestures of affection may be sensory in nature. Your son may find the light touch of your hand actually painful. As with all sensory issues, this can be worked on as long as you follow your child's lead. Working with deep pressure (see Q37 *'Why were we told to buy him a gym ball?'*) can help enormously. (See also Q19 *'Why won't he give me a hug?'*)

Giving your child control over how much and what sort of physical contact you share is vital. We most of us remember the distaste of some aunt or other such relative who insisted on hugging us to her bosom and kissing us when we really didn't want to go anywhere near her! Daft though it may sound, in our case we found that spending a lot of time lying around near our son - but not touching him - worked wonders. By lying down when he was sitting, kneeling or crouching, we ceased to be a threat and he could choose whether or not to approach us. Turning this into various games where he was in charge (his sitting on us, pinning us down, riding on our backs, tickling us etc.) moved on to a point where he is very tactile and openly affectionate. This (clearly) is nice for us, but is also useful for him. He is not defensive now about any touch and is able to sit in the middle of a group of people without minding if he is knocked into or jostled.

Whatever solution you eventually find to help your child *express* his affection, be assured that it is there. Having AS does not mean that you are unable to love. If you keep on loving him, and show it in a huge variety of ways (reading this book, for example, is a manifestation of it - it shows you care), he will love you back, however he may ultimately express it.

71. Do I really have to bother about all this when my son has AS so mildly?

Although (as usual!) there is no general agreement about this, increasingly it is becoming understood that there is no such thing as 'mild' Asperger syndrome. Just as you cannot be 'a little bit pregnant', so you cannot be 'a little bit autistic' or have 'just a touch of AS'. The term autism describes a neuro-developmental difference, and that difference is fact.

However, there most certainly is a huge variation in the *manifestation* of that autism. One person with autism may be profoundly affected, have no speech and be totally withdrawn, while another person may exhibit so few differences to the neuro-typical norm that his autism is barely detectable.

The pregnancy analogy may be useful here. Pregnancy is pregnancy - but the effect which it has on women differs hugely. One woman might sail through pregnancy never having felt better. She is full of energy, her skin is clear, her hair shines and is thick and glossy and she is generally happy, gregarious and confident throughout the nine months. Another woman (with the same condition - pregnancy) is seriously debilitated. She has no energy, she feels sick all the while, her muscles ache, she is clumsy, she becomes forgetful and irritable, she doesn't want to see anyone and spends the nine months as a virtual recluse.

In each example the condition is affecting the women in different ways, yet biologically they are experiencing the same changes. With autism (and Asperger syndrome) the same can be observed. One person with autism has sensory processing differences which mean that he cannot tolerate loud noises - yet another person with autism may crave sounds at high volume; one person may be so sensitive to touch that a rough label in the back of his shirt may be intolerable while another person may not realise that he has cut himself until he sees blood. There remain common misconceptions about autism. "He can't be autistic - he makes eye contact" is one. "Surely your son can't cope with the noise and stimulation of a theme park" is another. No two people with an identical diagnosis will be the same - yet the condition is. It is not that one person has 'mild' autism and another 'severe', but rather that one is *'mildly affected'* where for another the neuro-developmental effects are overwhelming.

To take the pregnancy parallel further: we could learn much from our acceptance of the 'difference' of pregnancy. Few women seem to emerge emotionally scarred by having 'had pregnancy'. Everyone knows that a pregnant woman may be nauseated by certain smells or that she may want to eat strange things. No one worries about this, in that the cause is known (i.e. she's pregnant.) On the whole these peculiarities are tolerated, even welcomed and celebrated. After all, she's not *ill*...

Asperger syndrome is not mild autism, and one person with AS is not 'more autistic' than the next. The difference is there, and may well be more profound than is realised, especially if the person with AS is managing the condition effectively. Most of the successful work with people with AS/autism is in the field of managing their condition - in accepting difference and then finding a way forward working with that difference. One of the other deciding factors in 'severity' may well be attitude. In our pregnancy analogy one woman was outgoing and confident because she knew she was beautiful, the other was withdrawn and unhappy because she believed that she was ugly. If we can encourage our children with AS to accept their AS, to enjoy it and celebrate it, how much more likely is it that they will be 'only mildly affected'?

72. If he's so clever, why is he doing so badly at school?

Whatever your son's level of intelligence, it is likely that he is brighter than he appears to be through his schoolwork. Underachievement at school is rife in children with AS. The fact that the child is having to cope in an often noisy, confusing, socially-orientated environment means that he has barriers to overcome before he can even begin to learn, and then the way the work is presented to him may be unsuitable. Much teaching relies initially on oral giving of information, which is then presented in a number of different ways, in different examples, to make sure that the concept has been grasped. Where this repetition may be helpful to many pupils, it is quite possibly confusing to a child with AS. In addition, it is not always made clear to the child exactly what learning is taking place, and the child with AS may have problems working out what learning has been inferred, and to generalise that learning across different contexts. Techniques which work to motivate and stimulate neuro-typical pupils (bright displays, surprises, group-negotiation, noise, movement, 'pace') may be confusing or even distressing to the child with AS. School, as an environment, is not a place which springs to mind as ideal for someone with AS, and many adults with AS tell of great unhappiness during their school years.

That said, it is possible to make schools more AS friendly, and a school which has a strong policy of Inclusion (rather than integration) should be willing to try to do this. This 'inclusion' needs to start with the child. You and your son's school together need to find out from your son why he is not doing well. It may be certain teachers, or certain classrooms which he finds difficult. It may be that he is overwhelmed by the whole day and is simply exhausted. It may be that one element (for example his slow writing, or his lack of organisation) is having a knock-on effect across the whole curriculum. Whatever the cause, it is for you, your son and the school to work together to make his education accessible to him. It is not good enough to say 'This is how we do it here'. Schools are required to be accessible to all pupils, to those with mobility problems who use wheelchairs through the installation of ramps and lifts, and to those with AS through different sorts of modification. (See also Q 89 *'Does he have to go to school?'*)

73. Why did she have to see all those specialists?

The diagnosis of AS is done through clinical observation. One element of this is though the elimination of other possibilities. Only when you are sure that your daughter has no hearing loss can you start to investigate her aural sensory sensitivity due to AS; only when you are sure that her eyesight is not at fault can you consider her use of eye contact. Even when other, more 'simple' possibilities have been ruled out, diagnosis of AS is a complex matter. It requires detailed and exact observation by highly qualified and experienced specialists. As yet there is no blood test or brain scan to diagnose autism (although these may be developed in the future.) It is a big diagnosis – you want to be sure it is right. Unfortunately it is still the case that some educational psychologists or paediatricians are giving a label of "assumed Asperger syndrome", often based on the shortest of interviews with the child, or even entirely on second-hand, anecdotal evidence. If you do not feel your child has been fully assessed, including having cognitive assessments and the 'ADOS' (Autistic Diagnostic Observation Schedule) – or similar, or has not been properly screened to make sure that the diagnosis is correct, you have the right to a fuller procedure. There are centres of excellence offering full and accurate diagnosis of Asperger syndrome, most noticeably, and nationally, the Social Communication Disorders Clinic at Great Ormond Street Hospital. A diagnosis, done properly, can take time and may involve many people, but it is reassuring to know that it is accurate. The NAS has some excellent fact sheets regarding diagnosis available to download from their website.

74. Are there any books on the subject I should encourage him to read?

There are many books *about* Asperger syndrome, most from a medical or educational viewpoint, but there are fewer written for the person with AS. A good one is 'Asperger syndrome, the universe and everything.' by Kenneth Hall who has AS himself, as does Luke Jackson who has written 'Freaks, Geeks and Asperger syndrome'. Others which are about children with AS are the 'Bluebottle Mystery' and others by Kathy Hoopman and of course, for older readers, the now classic 'The Curious Incident of the Dog in the Night-Time' by Mark Haddon. Adolescents may also be helped by reading the three Asperger Guides ('Personal', 'Social' and 'Love') by Genevieve Edmonds and Dean Worton, both adults with AS who take a very positive approach. More information about these can be found at the back of this book.

Always read autobiographical accounts first to ensure that the content is suitable for your child.

75. What difference does a label make?

I think many of us resist the label for as long as possible. There is something almost infinitely sad about landing your child with one defining feature, and a supposedly negative one at that. Perhaps you son *is* bright, *is* funny, *is* a boy, *has* brown hair, *has* a wicked chuckle…and he *is* also autistic and *has* Asperger syndrome. Many people feel quite strongly that individuals should be described as *having* a condition on the autistic spectrum rather than as *being* autistic. Semantics apart, the label still feels as if it is taking over.

Asperger syndrome is not your son's defining feature. He may be usually good, sometimes naughty, often cheeky, occasionally grumpy - the same as everyone else. It would be easy to attribute each of these, each time, to his having Asperger syndrome, and I don't think this would be either fair or true.

On the other hand, much of what he does is likely to be mysterious to you, in that he behaves and responds differently to other people. Your knowledge that he has a condition called Asperger syndrome can help you to understand him at these times. There are also legal implications in terms of being protected which are made far easier with a clear diagnostic label. Asperger syndrome is not a label to define your child, but it does give you a handle on much of what he feels and does.

76. Is he Gifted and Talented?

The arbitrary guidelines used to define this term seem to me rather sad. What 'gifted and talented' is taken to mean is: 'is his IQ within certain parameters?' or, 'is he exceptional?' Children with AS traditionally do rather poorer than their true level at IQ tests, so that - although probably fairer than judging on impression or school performance alone - this is probably still not a fair measure. And doesn't the fact that he has AS mean by definition that he is exceptional? At various points in this book, children with AS have been described as seeing things we don't see, hearing things we don't hear, having different memory abilities, having the fiercest concentration, inhabiting a different world. Of course your son is gifted and talented, although he may or may not fulfil the rather narrow criteria for that title as laid down by various organisations and departments. This is their loss, if he doesn't – not his. (See also Q96 *'Has she got any special talents?'*)

77. Is he dyslexic?

Possibly. Dyslexia and Asperger syndrome are different conditions, yet both provide barriers to academic learning for otherwise intelligent people, and both seem to indicate that the brain is working differently. Differently, not less well. It may seem a contradiction, but a child with AS who learned to read almost magically at the age of three, can still be dyslexic. He may find the deconstruction of sight-absorbed words impossible, so that he can read the word 'cataclysmic' and recognise instantly what it means, but could not tell you with what letter sound it begins. This lack of phonic understanding may be part of the reason why he is a poor writer. Another, also linked to dyslexia, may be a problem with spatial processing and organisation. Remembering the orientation of the actual letters can be a problem, as can the physical process of getting them down on paper (see Q6 *'Why can't she write?'*)

Your son may have both dyslexia and Asperger syndrome. My advice would be to investigate ways of supporting people with dyslexia and seeing if they help your son, rather than getting too hung up on another label. That said, a formal dyslexia diagnosis may grant him some advantages in education later, such as longer time in exams. It may be that, ultimately, you may have to pursue each condition separately.

78. Why is it that many of the symptoms I read about, I don't find in my son (who has the diagnosis), but in my neuro-typical daughter?

As far as I am aware, there are two major studies taking place at the moment looking into ASD characteristics in siblings of a child with an autism or Asperger diagnosis. Certainly, apocryphally, it seems that some aspects which specialists look for in a child suspected of autism, may actually come out instead in a brother or sister. Our daughter Elizabeth, for example, is a far pickier eater than Sam is, and for a long while would eat only things which were yellow (...and how autistic does that sound!) The point is that she has a highly developed social awareness, instinctively regulates her language depending on her audience, and interprets the subtlest of body and verbal language cues – and has done so from a very early age. Sam may be willing to eat a wider variety of food, but he doesn't really 'get' people – and that's why he is the one with the diagnosis of AS.

That said, having one child diagnosed with a condition on the autistic spectrum does make it more likely, statistically, that a sibling will also have a condition on the spectrum. Families may find that they have two, three, four – any number of children, all with an ASD. If you are worried about your daughter's social communication and interaction skills, it may be worth seeking an expert opinion. On the other hand, if you have no worries about her except that she likes to follow a certain path to school or to read the same book over and over again at bedtime, don't let your hyper-sensitivity to the autistic spectrum make you see problems which aren't there.

79. Does he know he's got Asperger syndrome?

The decision as to whether to tell your child about his diagnosis, or at least when to tell him, can be a tricky one. Many people are reluctant to share the label with a young child, at least until they have had time to become relaxed with the term themselves. On the other hand, you are going to have to make some explanation to your son as to why he is seeing so many specialists, and he may well already be hyper-sensitive to the belief that there is something 'wrong' with him. Understanding that he has a condition called Asperger syndrome, and that this at least largely explains why he is having the difficulties he is having, may well come as a huge relief to him. In addition to this it is worth considering that it is your child's right to understand who he is and this does include having an understanding that he has AS.

Luke Beardon, Senior Lecture in Autism at Sheffield Hallam University (who wrote the foreword to this book), says that there need to be five elements in place prior to 'breaking the news': "intellectual ability, cognitive ability, receptive communicative ability, motivation/interest, and post diagnostic support." He believes that these, rather than a specific age, should determine when the fact of the diagnosis should be shared.

We told Sam right from the beginning of investigations that the various doctors and specialists were interested in him because of his 'Special Brain'. Later he learned to call this his Asperger Brain, and he is immensely proud to have it. We have presented it to both our children, always, as a positive thing - to the extent that our daughter asked the final question in this book. Perhaps we have done too good a job…!

80. Should we tell Grandma and Granddad?

There have been many parents I have met who, when they told *their* parents were met with the response that a) there was nothing wrong with the child which a bit more discipline/firmness/fresh air/vegetables wouldn't fix and b) there's nothing odd about him because he's just like Uncle X was at his age (see Q 99 *'How did she get it?'*). Neither response is helpful. Of course, not all grandparents are the same and nor will be their response. Possibly just because AS has a genetic element, so that there is a feeling that it emerges from family rather than being completely random, it can be an emotive, difficult subject for the previous generation to absorb. Lorna Wing and Judith Gould only brought

Hans Asperger's work to general attention in 1979, so it is not something, yet, which grandparents will have come across in their own child-rearing experience. This in itself can lead to frustration and guilt that their own children were not given more support a generation ago. It may take another generation, when we who have been parents to children with a diagnosis of AS become grandparents, before full family groups are at ease with having Asperger syndrome amongst them.

81. What should we tell our friends?

Friends are a lot easier than family, precisely because they are not related by blood and are therefore out of the genetic equation. Also, although we all do (however seldom we admit it!) take a lively interest in how others raise their children and compare it to how we do so with ours, there isn't quite the same emotional intensity if we choose to do it differently to our friends, as if we choose to do it differently to our parents! It is likely that good friends will have been with you on the journey as you began to worry, began to suspect... eventually got a diagnosis for your child, so that the 'telling them' doesn't become an issue. More problematic is the knock-on effect of telling less good friends. We found we couldn't get a babysitter for months after our son was 're-categorised', although he was the same boy, who behaved in the same way as he had always done...

In the end, the whole issue of disclosure is a complicated one. Your son has the right to privacy, and, as someone with a hidden condition, the right to keep that private to himself if he chooses.

On the other hand, explaining about his AS is the only way to minimise misunderstandings and avoid trouble. On the whole, we have found that openness is our chosen path, on the basis that if you treat something like an embarrassing secret it is more likely to become one. It must, though, be an individual decision for each family. There is no right or wrong answer.

82. Will she have to go to a special school?

Indeed, *can* she go to a special school? There are a very limited number of schools which specialise for children with AS, together with a handful of specialised units. Much more likely is that you will be offered inclusion into mainstream for your daughter, possibly with the addition of a 'Statement' (Statement of Special Educational Needs). How you manage education is a subject for a book in its own right! It is worth, however, bearing in mind that Inclusion means the school adapting its environment and curriculum to accommodate your daughter's needs (with 'Integration' meaning that she adapts to fit their ways.) Education is a huge issue. See Q60 *'What should we do if she's bullied at school?'* Q72 *'If he's so clever, why is he doing so badly at school?'* and Q89 *'Does he have to go to school?'* for further comments on this subject.

83. Is he cleverer than our other children?

Of course, 'clever' has so many different interpretations. The answer to this will always be both a yes and a no; he will be cleverer in some ways, and less so in others. The important thing is to play always to strengths while at the same time supporting weaknesses.

Part of the diagnostic process for AS should be a series of IQ tests, and you may be pleased to find that your son with AS has an intelligence considerably above average. However, a potential disadvantage of this may be that you are aware of this and can quantify it, whereas your other children who do not have AS have to get by with the usual measures of SATS results, school setting and so on. It may seem a little unfair (particularly to the siblings!) that your child with AS has a number he can bandy around to prove he is bright when they, his brothers or sisters, do not. However, your son with AS needs this evidence more than other children do, having other hurdles in the way of his brightness being obvious. Family dynamics are interesting, though, and this problem was not one which we had anticipated or were expecting. Sometimes, it seems, even good news can lead to difficulties!

84. How do we stop our other children feeling left out?

Asking this question is an answer in itself. If you are aware that your other children are likely to feel left out by your overwhelming concern for your child with AS you are likely also to take care to reassure them that you still have time for them. It can be tough to be merely 'normal'; make sure you make your other children feel special too.

And while we're on the subject, try to keep some time and attention for your partner too - and, just as important, for yourself. This 'problem' (which perhaps isn't such a problem after all) is going to be around for a long time. Pace yourself!

85. Will he ever have a girlfriend?

I suppose what this question means is, will he ever be a social success? Will he ever be attractive, to the other or indeed his own sex? I think the key to this is not whether he has Asperger syndrome, but whether having Asperger syndrome has led to damage to his self-esteem. There are plenty of people who are different in some way who remain highly attractive, and enjoy high social standing. Indeed, beyond the early teen years, when being the same as the crowd is the socially accepted norm, many people work very hard to appear different or interesting. The person with Asperger syndrome has an advantage here, since he sees the world differently and has the inside track on being 'quirky'. Sadly, if this is allied with a feeling that he is a failure, that his way is wrong, that his peers have rejected him then his self-perception is likely to be pretty low, with a resulting drop in "sex appeal". If, on the other hand, he is brim-full of confidence, enjoys his difference and is happy to be who he is, then that is likely to be pretty attractive – to everyone. There are plenty of Asperger marriages; of course he will have a girlfriend, if he wants one, as long as he is not too knocked about by the world in the meantime.

86. When will he learn that we're joking?

Curiously, jokes can become something of a special interest to children with AS. Puns, and the juxtaposition of two things in an unexpected way, can be hugely amusing. You may find you have a 'Knock, Knock' joke king on your hands!

Other jokes, which involve social intricacies, are more tricky, and are likely to mean nothing to your son. Mr Bean, to the individual with AS, can make absolute sense!

The problem with the phrase "I was joking" is that it can be used to mask teasing and cruelty. A joke is not a joke if it is not amusing to the appropriate parties. This will probably have to be explained quite overtly to your son. If A says something about B and B thinks it is funny but C does not, that is a joke (as long as B is really amused and not laughing to cover embarrassment - but that's a whole other area!); if A says something about B and C thinks it is funny, but B does not, then it is not a joke. Jokes are complicated. Your son is vulnerable as the person who doesn't get the joke, and as the subject of the joke and also as the maker of the joke. His jokes may come across as merely rude.

As to whether he will ever learn that you are joking, that depends. Most people 'get' that someone is joking by reading subtle facial expressions. These may have to be rather more overt for your son. People with AS can certainly have a sense of humour. Like all things, it may not be quite the same as for the neuro-typical population.

87. What can we do all together as a family?

There may be things your child with AS chooses to avoid. If, for example, the noise and sensory stimulation of the swimming pool is uncomfortable to him, clearly this does not make sense for a family outing. On the other hand, if going swimming is your neuro-typical daughter's absolute favourite family trip, stopping is going to lead (quite naturally) to resentment.

It may be that you cannot do some things as a family, and that you need to split into groups, or let your other children go with friends. On the other hand, there are still things you can do - specifically anything you all enjoyed doing before receiving a diagnosis. Having a label hasn't changed your child. If he hated going swimming before, then it probably wasn't much of a family treat anyway. If he loved it, then knowing he has AS (and reading in your 'Guide to Asperger syndrome' leaflet that some children with AS do not enjoy it) does not change anything. All children with AS are different. Trust your child, not some fictitious 'Asperger norm'.

88. Does he have an imagination

The three elements used by Lorna Wing to define autism (the so-called "triad of Impairment") are an impairment of Social Relationships, an impairment of Social Communication and an impairment of Social Understanding or Imagination. This use of the word 'imagination' has led to the misperception that people with AS have poor imagination. This is not (necessarily) the case.

"Social imagination" could perhaps be re–described as "social empathy", the ability to understand what another is thinking or feeling. This is not what is commonly meant by imagination. It is possible a person with AS may have an unusually highly developed ability to occupy an imaginary world. This ability in some people with AS to 'tune out' the world around them and instead to retreat to another place is striking. It is quite likely that your son has a potent imagination. Indeed, it may be so strong that at times it rivals – and even takes over from – the physical world around him.

89. Does he have to go to school?

The law in England and Wales (Scotland is subtly different, although broadly the same) is that a child needs to be educated, full time, from the beginning of the term following his fifth birthday until he reaches the age of sixteen (soon to rise to eighteen, if news reports are to be believed). This can take place in school – *or otherwise.* As long as you are prepared to make sure that your son receives a full time education (and what that education should be is open to huge variations of interpretation), he does not need to go to school.

Taking him out of school is obviously an enormous step, but awareness that you can do so can be an almost unfathomable relief to parents and child with AS who have struggled on and on in an unsupportive system. School does, undoubtedly, present huge potential difficulties for the child with AS. Many schools work long hours tirelessly to try to make school more appropriate for a child with AS. Some succeed. Others do not always have so positive approach, and you may find yourself bashing against a wall as you try to make the school understand your son's needs, and be flexible enough to try to meet them. At some point, as you watch your son facing an inappropriate environment - where he may be unhappy, learning little and be, in fact, unsafe - the awareness that *he needn't go* can be a lifesaver. The organisations Education Otherwise and HEAS (see contact details given at the back of this book) offer support and information to anyone wishing to take a child out of school. You do not have to be a teacher, nor to have any specific academic qualifications. It is still possible to take a full range of exams from out of the school system, or not, just as you choose. Home educating a child is not for everyone, nor is it, in itself, an end to all problems. However, it is an option - one of which not everyone is aware - and it may well be one that your child with AS, if left to his own devices, would choose unhesitatingly. (See Q 60 *'What should we do if she's bullied at school?'* and Q72 *'If he's so clever, why is he doing so badly at school'*)

90. Doesn't he care when I cry?

Many young children with AS seem to have little concept of crying as an expression of distress. Our son commented that I had "water coming out of my eyes". More importantly, children with AS seem to have no understanding that another person's distress may have a relevance to them.

Diplomacy in this can, of course, be taught. It is possible to teach a child what sadness looks like, and to practice some models of appropriate behaviour when it is encountered. For example, you could teach 'if another child falls down in the playground and cries, squat down beside him and say, "Are you alright?"' (Bear in mind that if you are to teach this it is useful also to teach that he should listen to the reply!)

Whether this is ever translated into real concern is debatable. Part of the nature of AS is this inability to empathise with how another person is feeling. Certainly it will take time and practice, and some complex work on practical suggestions. It will also take work on the fact that sympathy can offer comfort, even if it gives no practical help. Most of us have felt that impotent feeling of helplessness when someone is upset, hurt, bereaved. There is, literally, nothing we can do to help. The idea that doing nothing *does* (somehow) help is one which most of us find very hard to fully grasp. It may be that, for a person with AS, the same concept, that somehow sympathy can help even when of no practical benefit, is just even harder to grasp still.

91. Wasn't he sad when Granny died?

There are different aspects to sadness - feeling it and expressing it. It may be that a child with AS has trouble feeling sadness, or it may be that he merely has trouble expressing sadness.

Death is likely to be approached more prosaically by someone with AS than by most. After all, it is inevitable, it is a natural part of the life cycle and it is to be expected, especially if someone is old or ill. The process of the heart stopping beating, the cells dying, even decomposition are all subjects which may well fascinate a child with AS, and although his expressions of them may seem inappropriate, they are not intended to be. Death is interesting.

Loss, on the other hand, is more mysterious. A person with AS is likely to feel loss just as acutely as anyone else (indeed perhaps more so in that it is change on a fundamental level), although he may not have the communication skills to express it, nor the emotional dexterity to understand it himself. It should not be assumed that, just because he does not express sadness, a person with AS is not experiencing bereavement as acutely as anyone else.

92. Doesn't he care what he looks like?

The way people use their appearance as a piece of social currency may be missed by someone with AS. Even if he is aware that others are saying something about themselves by what they wear and how their hair is groomed, it may be that a person with AS struggles to have a strong enough self-image to be able to project it in this way.

If your son chooses what he wears primarily for comfort it may be that you have to intervene to a certain extent if he is to conform to the social norm. It is possible to upset people culturally by 'dressing inappropriately', and this may need to be explained to your son.

Ultimately, though, you need to be aware that if you continue to choose his clothes that this, too, may show. If he lacks the personal confidence and understanding to choose an 'image' for himself, and lacks the peer support which would otherwise help him in this, it might be a kindness to at least let someone his age help you to choose his clothes. As with the need for personal hygiene, he may not care but other people do, and it is part of the job of supporting him to help him present as socially acceptable a face to the world as he can, and that needs to be socially acceptable to *his* generation rather than to yours. (See also Q67 *'Should I let her wear what she wants?'*)

That said, it is just possible that the clothes he chooses *are* his expression of identity. "Don't you care what you look like?" is an irrelevant parental refrain. If he does care what he looks like, then whether you agree with him is, I'm afraid, not the point!

93. Could moving abroad be the answer?

This is a fascinating question for someone trying to 'manage' AS. Many of the social problems of AS are, after all, because the person is trying to make sense of a society governed by largely implied, infinitely fluctuating rules. Yet, if the person moves abroad to a very different culture, these rules may become overt and any lapses may well be put down to 'being a foreigner', rather than to Asperger syndrome. Some cultures, like for example that of Japan, have a formalised social culture where the rules can be learned and, if followed, 'correct' behaviour is guaranteed. It may sound an eccentric solution, but moving abroad could quite possibly be a very real answer for a person with AS.

94. Is he entitled to any benefits?

Once you have come to terms with the concept of AS in your child, you are in a position to explore benefits. For many parents, the fact that these benefits fall under the 'disability' umbrella is off-putting. It can be hard, while you're still reeling from the news that your child has a 'syndrome', to cope with the language that he has a 'disability' as well.

The Disability Living Allowance is one of the benefits which is worth exploring for children with AS. When you look at the questions you realise that actually, yes - he does need more supervision than other children his age, that yes - he does need help with communication, and yes - he does need support if he is to access sports and activities freely available to others his age. Filling the form in can be useful not only because it may lead to financial help (which, given the extra work which bringing up a child with AS successfully can entail is likely to be very useful), but also because it can help you quantify just how your child's needs are different from those of other children his age. Your understanding of this doesn't make him any more (or less) 'disabled', it just makes you more consciously aware of his needs. Whether the benefits are forthcoming will depend on each individual case, but certainly children with AS may qualify and it is an avenue worth exploring.

95. Will he get to university?

We all of us play this game with our children, often right from when they are tiny babies: Will he be a football player? Will he be a musician? Will he go to university?

Having AS is not (clearly!) a guarantee that you son will have a higher education (although the diagnosis does suggest an at least average and quite likely an above or well above-average IQ.) If he is bright enough, or perhaps more relevantly if he does well enough at school or in examinations, there is no reason why he shouldn't go to university. More and more universities are becoming aware of the need to provide inclusion services to young people with Asperger syndrome. These include preview of material at lectures, use of a scribe to take notes, help with organising and managing workload and a peer support system to help with the inevitable social pressures. Universities are increasingly aware that many very bright students with AS are a huge asset to them, if given a little support. The future, at least in higher education, seems bright.

96. Has she got any special talents?

One of the irritations of autism is that the media has always had a fascination with what have been termed 'Savants', people with autism who also possess astonishing 'islands' of skill or talent. Films such as 'Rainman' have not helped this perception that having autism must inevitably mean that the person also has a hidden 'gift'. This is only very rarely the case.

Having said that, there are many elements of the way the brain works in autism and AS which are not yet fully understood. For example, one of the elements which has been only fairly recently understood is the extent to which individuals may perceive the world through their senses in a different way. These sensory processing differences mean that your daughter may see things you don't see or hear things you don't hear. This may, of course, result in distress, and awareness of sensory difference is one of the more important elements of understanding and helping people with conditions on the autistic spectrum. However, it may also result in advantages. A person with AS may be aware of the shape of images and to separate these shapes from the 'whole' of the picture. Sometimes this may result in quite astonishing artwork. Similarly, a person with AS may have a different system for filing and retrieving memories. She may have a particularly strong ability to memorise phrases, reproducing them exactly as heard (complete with accent!), without necessarily having much interest in their intrinsic meaning. This may result in ability to remember musical phrases with the same accuracy...

These 'quirks' are certainly not unusual in people with conditions on the autistic spectrum, and if viewed affectionately and with appreciation, they can be a huge help preserving self-esteem. We all need to find things we are good at. Your daughter may or may not have particular 'odd' special talents. Certainly it is worth looking out for what she is good at, because it may be something which would otherwise be missed by conventional education. Whether unusual or not, your daughter *will* have talents, and concentrating on what she is good at, rather than on her supposed 'deficits' has got to be a positive approach. (See Q76 *'Is he Gifted and Talented?'*)

97. Should we forget about Christmas?

There is much in Christmas (or any other major family or religious festival) which makes it a problem for someone with AS. As already mentioned in Q32 (*'Why does he have to spoil every big event?'*), usual routines change, people come to stay, meal times are different and may involve different foods, certain clothes may be worn, new toys are received but there isn't space or time to play with them... and generally there tends to be a level of stress in the air which is upsetting for many children with AS. As a result the child with AS tries to go off by himself, gets into trouble for being anti-social, refuses to eat the family dinner, tells Uncle Jim that his present is the wrong sort, won't give Auntie May a goodbye kiss, has a tantrum, hits his brother ...and his parents are left in despair!

In the face of this, cancelling family festivals may seem like a good idea, but in fact all is needed is to have your child with AS's needs addressed. If, rather than opening ten presents he would be happier opening one and then being allowed to go off and play with it, perhaps this can be arranged. If his favourite food is cold baked beans on a separate plate to hot mashed potatoes, this doesn't seem impossible to accommodate into the family dinner. In other words, your child has Asperger syndrome all year round. It is unrealistic to expect him to stop having it, or to stop showing any symptoms of it, just at the time you are adding in other stresses. Start with planning an AS-friendly festival for one member of your family, and then see just how much you can add in, without disruption, for everyone else. It *can* still be a happy day!

Section Four: The big questions

....

98. Will he get better?

(This is a big question, perhaps THE big question, and it is not one on which everyone agrees. It is probably only fair to say that the same question may get a different response in different literature.)

Asperger syndrome is a lifelong, neuro-developmental condition. The term describes an aspect of how your son is, and of how his brain works. You can't "get better" from how you are and nor, quite likely, would your son wish to, nor even wish that his brain worked differently.

What he might wish is that whatever 'problem' led to him, you or somebody seeking a diagnosis, it would 'get better'. There are likely to have been elements in his life which were going wrong which prompted you to seek a diagnosis. For example, the diagnosis may have been suggested because he was unhappy, anxious, failing at school, self-harming, failing to communicate, socially isolated… and these things most definitely *can* get better than they are now. Many of the answers in this book relate to these ways of 'getting better'.

'Getting better' does not mean 'cured'. Your son has Asperger syndrome, and that is not going to change. My hope is that, as you have journeyed through this book, you have come to a point where you no longer see a reason to want to change this in him. I believe that Asperger syndrome is a difference, and is only a disability if the problems caused by having this difference are not addressed.

Having said that, far from getting better it may actually seem at times as if your son's AS is getting worse. Having Asperger syndrome is a roller-coaster ride. Just when you feel you've got your thinking around it and have headed-off one set of problems, a completely new set is likely to raise its head. This is largely because the person with AS - your son - is growing up, changing, and therefore the social environment in which he operates is changing too. You work with him on sharing toys, only to find that the world has moved on and he needs to learn about music trends. You may never catch up!

More complicated still is that, as he grows towards adolescence, social rules become intensely important, almost entirely implied and fiercely subtle. Adolescents seldom say what they mean, nor mean what they say on a surface level. Many interchanges are to do, at some level, with social pecking-order, and may also be governed by rules of attraction and attractiveness. We who are a generation on are never going to get these exchanges right (almost by definition!), and so we cannot help our AS children to navigate through this time. AS may 'get worse' in adolescence because it becomes a serious disadvantage to have a social deficit at this most socially conscious time of life.

It is through the time of secondary school that individuals with AS are most likely to feel isolated, be ostracised or bullied and to have their self-esteem damaged. Depression, in adolescents with AS, is so prevalent that there was a recent study (Hare, 2005) to see whether it is actually a symptom of the condition. The good news is that the conclusion is that it is not – it is just an extremely common by-product of a person with AS trying to manage a non-AS environment.

Therefore, although AS does not get worse, it could fairly be said that it may get worse to have it, at least for a while. All that can be done is to protect the person as far as possible and weather the storm. The day when individuality is valued will come again (usually around the 18-year-old mark), and if you can protect your son's perception of himself there is no reason why he can't emerge from the 'hell' of growing up happy to be who he is, AS and all.

So, is there a cure?
No.

You may think that rather a blunt answer, but it is one which I believe it is essential to get into your head. A great deal of time, energy and emotion (not to mention money) can be wasted chasing that particular rainbow. There is, at least at the moment, no cure for autism.

There are treatments. Some target specifics, rather than the autism itself. For example, Sensory Integration Therapy targets the sensory differences which are found frequently in individuals with conditions on the autistic spectrum, providing a therapeutic programme to help with this specific aspect of the condition. Others attempt to deal more with elements which may be exacerbating the condition, for example by targeting toxicity or by altering diet. Yet others try to alleviate symptoms, for example by correcting visual disturbance through the use of coloured lenses. (See details given at the back of this book). There is probably a great deal of good in a great many of these, and it must be for each individual, and for individual families to decide which and when to try. There is a considerable body of people who believe that different treatments have made huge differences to their lives or to the life of their child, and such testaments should not be dismissed lightly. Anything so positive should not be dismissed out of hand, particularly when medical science is still so unsure of the causes or even of the manifestations of autism.

A realistic approach is probably to forget about curing your child's AS (he quite likely would not thank you for it anyway), and to concentrate instead on 'curing' the things which are causing him and you distress. Look at his diet, his environment, at the way you interact with him... Work on the symptoms which distress you or him, but don't forget to celebrate the things about him - possibly just as much symptoms of AS - which are great.

Having said there is no cure, there are two main treatments which you will come across which actually target the autism itself in the child. The first is ABA (Applied Behaviour Analysis - or Lovaas after the Doctor who pioneered it) and the second is the Sonrise Programme from the Autism Treatment Centre of America. Both make huge claims to success, and your decision as to whether to follow either will need to be based on considerable research. In the briefest summary (which can hardly do either justice), ABA targets - and claims to reduce or even eliminate - autistic behaviour by breaking behaviour into small steps and consistently rewarding that which is desired. Sonrise is in many ways the complete opposite, accepting autistic behaviour and instead concentrating overwhelmingly on social interaction. Both programmes make huge demands on time, commitment and money. Both have many people who have followed them and who believe passionately in the results. It would be naïve to dismiss them as irrelevant (though it is also true that other people have tried them and report no effect whatsoever). The only thing to do is to find out about them for yourself (see contact details given at the back of this book). Whether to believe in them, and to subscribe to them, really must be a strictly personal decision for each family, since it is in some ways a potentially life-changing decision. No one can, or should, tell you what to do.

99. How did she get it?

When we find there is something "wrong" with our child it is perhaps natural to want a reason. Is it something I did? Is it something that was done to her, like an inoculation for example, or something she has been eating? Is it genetic - in which case does it come through my family or his?

To date, there are no easy answers. Scientists are growing increasingly sure that there is a genetic element in autism, but that it is not as simple as being 'inherited' from mother or father. It seems more that some families carry a genetic vulnerability, and that added to this an element of environmental influence can somehow "switch on" this genetic predisposition. What these environmental factors may be continues to be the subject of heated debate, and may well become clearer in the next few years.

In time, no doubt, the debate about where autism comes from will be decided, as will the other argument about whether it is becoming more prevalent, or only appearing to be so through more accurate diagnosis. Neither of these answers, though, is likely to benefit your daughter at the moment. Hard though it is, the question "why?" may need to be laid aside in preference for "What now?"

However, even looking firmly forward does not solve the potential complications of this question. After all, if scientists believe that there is a genetic element in autism, does that mean that your grandchildren are likely to be more vulnerable to it?

This genetic link does appear to be quite strong. What this means is that many families who have a child diagnosed with AS are able to look back through the relatives and identify characteristics in other family members. ("So THAT'S why Great Uncle Albert was so odd!") Many people identify elements of AS in themselves, too, and more adults are coming forward for diagnosis as a result of this increased awareness.

There is, therefore, a possibility that your children may find that their children have AS too – but it is only a possibility. Nor is this automatically a negative thing. One of the positives of all this is that your child is likely to have been born into a family who views at least some of her AS behaviour as a family norm, and this can be a huge help. You may find that she forms a particularly strong bond with, for example, her grandfather, who is otherwise noticeably gauche around children and has always been a 'bit of a loner'. They may pursue their fascination with classification of pond life together in happy, silent accord...

100.How bad is it?

For much of this book you will have found a very positive tone about Asperger syndrome. This does not mean that I do not think that it is serious.

A diagnosis of Asperger syndrome is indeed serious. It is so because, if nothing is done to support the person, having AS can have a shattering impact on the individual. Without support he (or she) may be socially isolated and feel a social failure, may suffer from loneliness and depression, may underachieve massively at school, may fail to attain qualifications, may not manage to find or keep work, may suffer anxiety and feelings of worthlessness, may find him or herself in trouble with the law... may, in fact, find that he or she struggles to live successfully.

These are the potential negative sides of Asperger syndrome, but there is nothing inherent in the condition that means that any of these is inevitable. An understanding of AS, initially in the family and professionals supporting the child, and ultimately in the individual him or herself, can make all the difference. The over-riding tone of this book is positive because, once AS has been identified and understood, I do not believe that it need be negative.

I think that one of the most difficult issues when coming to terms with an AS diagnosis for your child is that of trying to work out how 'serious' it is. We found that no-one could really answer that - that no-one seemed prepared to give us an indication of whether this was an incidental 'bolt-on' to his life (like finding out he was left-handed, or that he had imperfect vision) or whether it was the fundamental, life defining element which would most shape his future. We wanted to know if he will ever leave home. We wanted to know if he will grow up and live independently, his AS just a quirk in his nature, or if he will always need care. We wanted to know, "How bad is it?"

Each child receiving a diagnosis of Asperger syndrome is, of course, different, as are the conditions which led to his diagnosis. One may be a happy, until then apparently typically-functioning four-year-old who has been picked up by a Speech and Language Therapist through his unusually developing semantics; another may be a troubled fourteen year old, already excluded from school, in trouble with the police and identified by a psychiatrist assessing suicidal tendencies. Clearly, although the diagnosis is the same, the level of distress the condition has caused is not.

I believe that there is nothing intrinsic in having AS which excludes a fully independent, happy, fulfilled life, including a completed education, a rewarding job and a full family life. Having AS can put hurdles in the way of the individual attaining these goals, but they can be overcome. It is much more important to focus on ways over the hurdles than to get hung up on the fact that they are there. There is an increasing range of supports for people who are left-handed; vision can be corrected by wearing glasses or contact lenses. Having AS can be compensated for, and the condition managed and even celebrated.

...and Section Five:

....

101. Why can't I have Asperger syndrome?

When I was gathering the original questions for this book, this was the first question which our daughter Elizabeth came up with. It is poignant, carrying as it does all the frustration of a 'normal' child faced with a 'different' sibling, but it is also quite profound. Our son Sam would certainly not choose otherwise than to have AS. Our daughter envies him. Why then did we ever see it as a problem?

Having a disability diagnosed in your child is devastating, and it is completely understandable that the parents immediately look to see how they can 'put it right', how they can protect and support their child and how they can prevent all the bad things which they know the diagnosis can mean. We read that perhaps as many as half the teenagers with an AS diagnosis suffer from clinical depression; we hear that the prison population is disproportionately full of people with an ASD; we see cases of people socially isolated, without work, friends or family and we fear for our children. We are all too aware of what the diagnosis means if it all goes wrong.

Yet there is a growing wave of people with AS who are objecting to the 'disability' label. As the first wave of children to whom this diagnosis was given reach adulthood, they are starting to have a very definite voice. It is a voice which is demanding not to be patronised. As a group of people they may be different in some ways to the larger population, but how is it that the larger population can assume that these differences are automatically 'wrong'? Many people with AS are beginning to demand that their different learning styles be catered for in education, and that they be respected. There is a growing body of university graduates with AS who are demanding that we respect that this so called *disability* is in actual fact an *ability*. Why do we still say "suffering from Asperger syndrome"? Why not turn that around and at least entertain the possibility that our son or daughter, far from suffering from a disability, is in fact benefiting from a gift?

I can honestly say that I don't know whether (if it were possible) I would choose to have Asperger syndrome. It takes a finer imagination than mine to be able to understand what that would mean, to be able to comprehend just how different the world would seem. How we perceive the world is ultimately a very personal thing. Who is to say that my reality is the same as yours? Perhaps we are already all more 'different' than we realise.

I do, though, honestly believe now that I would not (if it were possible) choose that my son did not have Asperger syndrome. I have stopped believing that his AS is somehow an enemy, like a germ attacking him and preventing him from being himself. Instead I believe that 'having Asperger syndrome' is just one more way of describing the infinite possibilities of who he is. It is a part of being him.

...and he's fine, just as he is.

I hope this book has answered at least some of your questions and has helped you as you set off on you Asperger journey. I wish you courage as you take your first steps, energy to keep going forward, a sense of humour to enjoy the scenery… and the very best of luck!

Clare Lawrence.

Useful contacts and further information:

Dr Tony Attwood
Web site: www.tonyattwood.com
Books: Asperger's Syndrome: a guide for parents and professionals (Jessica Kingsley Publications, 1998. ISBN 1 853 02 577 1). Although this was written eight years ago, it remains the 'must-read' book on AS. Dr Attwood has written many other books on the subject since, most recently **The Complete Guide to Asperger Syndrome**. He also comes back from Australia regularly to give talks - if you get the chance, go to one!

Social Stories
Carol Gray's technique for teaching the management of social situations to young people with ASD. **Web Site:** www.thegraycentre.org **Books** include **the New Social Story Book** (Future Horizons inc. ISBN 1 885 477 66 X)

Diet
Some web sites with information on the gluten/casein free diet are:
www.gfcfdiet.com **or** www.autismmedical.com

Vitamins etc
Current research for this takes place at the University of Sunderland **Web site:** www.osaris.sunderland.ac.uk

Recommended books for people with AS
Freaks, Geeks and Asperger syndrome - a User Guide to Adolescence by Luke Jackson (Jessica Kingsley, 2002. ISBN: 1 843 10 098 3

Blue Bottle Mystery: An Asperger Adventure by Kathy Hoopmann (Jessica Kingsley, 2001. ISBN: 1 853 02 978 5)
Asperger syndrome, the universe and everything by Kenneth Hall (Jessica Kingsley, 2001. ISBN: 1 853 02 930 0)
The Curious Incident of the Dog in the Night-Time by Mark Haddon (Jonathan Cape, 2003. ISBN: 0 224 06378 2)
The Asperger Love Guide/Personal Guide/Social Guide by Genevieve Edmonds and Dean Worton
(Karnac Books)

Home Education
Support and information on taking your child out of the school system can be found at **Education Otherwise, PO Box 325, King's Lynn. PE34 3XW** www.education-otherwise.org and at **The Home Education Advisory Service (HEAS), PO Box 98, Welwyn Garden City, Herts. AL8 6AN** www.heas.org.uk

Treatments and programmes
Information on Irlen Lenses can be found at **The Irlen Institute** www.irlen.com
Information on **Sensory Integration Therapy** can be found at the web site of **Sensory Integration International** at www.sensoryint.com and the **National Autistic Society** (www.nas.org) has a useful information sheet on the subject entitled **The Sensory World of the Autistic Spectrum**

Information on **A.B.A. (Applied Behavioural Analysis)** can be found via the **Lovaas Institute** website at www.lovaas-.com **www.lovaas,com** and about the **Son-**

Rise Program from the **Autism Treatment Centre of America** at www.autismtreatmentcenter.org

Diagnosis

Professional and accurate diagnosis of Asperger syndrome is provided nationally through the **Social Communication Disorders Clinic, Great Ormond Street Hospital, London WC1N 3JH.** There are other centres locally around the country (**The Fleming Nuffield Unit** in **Newcastle**, for example, offers an excellent service to the north-east of the country), and a varying degree of expertise and experience in various doctors, paediatricians and psychologists. The National Autistic Society (www.nas.org) should be able to help you if you are having trouble getting a full and proper diagnosis for your child.